3 0012 00040077

D1179041

Easy
BORDERS

WITHDRAWN FROM STOCK

WITHDRAWN FROM STOCK

high-performance
plans
for low-maintenance
gardens

Easy
BORDERS

MOLLY
EPHRAUMS

G7868

LIMERICK
635
963
COUNTY LIBRARY

David & Charles

For James, Melanie and Edward

A DAVID & CHARLES BOOK

First Published in the UK 1995

Copyright © Molly Ephraums 1995

Molly Ephraums has asserted her right to be identified as author of this work
in accordance with the Copyright, Designs and Patents Act, 1988.

All rights reserved. No part of this publication may be reproduced, stored in
a retrieval system, or transmitted, in any form or by any means, electronic or
mechanical, by photocopying, recording or otherwise, without prior
permission in writing from the publisher.

A catalogue record for this book is available from the British Library.

ISBN 0 7153 0316 3

Book design by Diana Knapp
Typeset by ABM Typographics Ltd, Hull
and printed in Italy by Lego SpA
for David & Charles
Brunel House   Newton Abbot   Devon

CONTENTS

Introduction

The truth about the bad habits of some plants is not always readily available, but it is essential to know which ones are well behaved if you want an easy-to-manage garden. This book will provide all the information you need to choose and grow plants that are non-invasive and trouble-free.

INTRODUCTION

Of all the sayings frequently quoted, there are two that experienced gardeners will treat with a certain measure of scepticism. These are: 'A thing of beauty is a joy for ever' and 'Hard work never killed anyone'. However, that 'One learns by experience' they will assure you is true. Had *I* known years ago what I know now I would have saved myself a great deal of disappointment, frustration and hard work. Wiser now, I hope to pass on the experience gathered over many years in the hope that this book will help you avoid the mistakes I made, and will be a guide to choosing a range of plants that will prove to be as trouble free in your garden as they have been in mine.

Twenty-five years ago I began the restoration of a derelict cottage garden, in which the remains of two herbaceous borders affected me in much the same way as two abandoned strays would affect a devoted dog-lover. Filled with compassion for these horticultural waifs, I embarked on their rescue with all the ignorance and enthusiasm of the uninitiated. Unaware of the consequences of my actions, and determined to restore the borders to health and beauty in the shortest possible time, I set to work, digging, clearing, and rescuing the few plants that survived among the weeds.

Restrained only by limited funds, I turned to kind friends, who responded, as all keen gardeners do, with generous gifts of off-shoots and divided clumps of perennials. Too late, I learnt the most important lesson of all, which is: If people have plants to spare it usually means they have too many of them. In other words, what you are being offered has come, in all probability, from a plant that has become too large, or invasive. Of course this is not always so – all of us have had

our gardens enriched by the generous person who insists on presenting us with a cutting or root of one of their most rare and precious plants – but in general it is essential to qualify your acceptance of the plant with a gentle interrogation as to its habits and eventual size. If I have learnt one thing it is to treat all offerings with polite mistrust until I have had time to read, research and, above all, consult my experienced friends on the advisability of allowing this newcomer into my garden.

Within a few years I had become sadder and wiser; the little clumps I had received with such pleasure and gratitude had repaid my hospitality not only by establishing their rights to new territory, but also by showing every sign of taking it over completely. With roots that invaded and dominated adjoining residents, seedlings that established squatters' rights in any vacant space, and enthusiastic new arrivals which overwhelmed their neighbours with an all enveloping embrace, I battled to maintain two borders that were rapidly getting out of control.

Sadly, I realised that a firm hand was needed; beautiful they might be but their manners left a great deal to be desired; some inhabitants would have to be evicted. This was not always easy. With the tenacity of those who have established themselves firmly in an area much to their liking and have no wish to be moved on, many proved extremely difficult to uproot. The length, and strength, of the roots of some perennial plants came as something of a surprise, not to mention a shock, to a novice gardener.

Those two borders led me to write this book, which is designed to help those of you who wish to enjoy your garden, but do not have the space or time to maintain a traditional, labour-intensive herbaceous

PAGE 6:
This herbaceous border enhances the corner of the garden.

border. It is also a guide for those of you who, like myself, are restricted by the physical limitations of advancing years, and wish to adapt your existing beds or borders by substituting some of the more difficult perennials with a selection of low maintenance plants which will require the minimum of attention.

Most of us lead busy lives and although modern gardens do tend to be modest in size we have to manage with little or no help in maintaining them. As we grow old we can no longer undertake on our own the heavy work such as lifting and dividing large, overgrown clumps of perennials. Ready-to-plant annuals get more expensive every year and not everyone has the time, or the facilities, to raise their own. Also, the majority of us want a reasonable supply of flowers and foliage for cutting, and flower arrangers demand a wide selection of material which cannot be supplied by annuals alone.

Hardy perennials (see box) can provide the solution.

There is a vast range of hardy perennials available in every size, form and colour and it must be stressed that their growing habits vary from the well disciplined to the unmanageable, so great caution and restraint needs to be exercised when making a selection. Carefully chosen perennials require very little attention, it is all too easy, however, as I found to my cost, to be carried away by the tantalising variety on offer, and find, too late, that the bed or border you have created is no longer a joy to behold, but has become so demanding of your time that you have insufficient energy left for the rest of your garden.

In the Directory of Easy Perennials (p.66) I have listed perennials which I have found to have impeccable manners and none of the bad habits and excesses to which many of their more exuberant bedfellows are prone. Some are well known and easily available, others are less common but are well worth tracking down. Many can be raised from seed should you wish to grow your own plants. Although the lists are not completely exhaustive they have been compiled from my own experience and I hope they will encourage you to try some of these well-behaved plants in your garden and discover how rewarding they can be.

Almost all the plants listed in the Directory are ones that I have grown and found to be exemplary, but there are one or two that I have not, as yet, been able to fit into my redesigned borders. These have been observed in the gardens of trusted friends, and have been endorsed by them as being of good behaviour.

Aware that we all have different-sized gardens, not to mention different views on what constitutes good manners, I have made a selection of perennials that I can best describe as 'borderline' cases for the easy border. Some people are more tolerant of wayward behaviour than others and I certainly do not want to deter you from trying out a large range of perennials but, if you wish to reduce the time and effort expended on maintaining your garden, you will need to be aware of the dangers inherent in a random selection.

In the Borderline Directory (p.92) I have listed those plants that I consider to be worthy of inclusion but which do require some degree of control and extra attention, for example, the larger hostas. These will prove entirely trouble free, unless you are inflicted with a great many slugs, but can grow into very large clumps after 4–6 years, which may then have to be lifted and divided, depending on where they are and how large you are prepared to allow them to grow.

After the Borderline Directory there are two further lists: selections of shrubs and bulbs for easy mixed borders.

READING BETWEEN THE LINES

It is all too easy to forget, when faced with some fascinating and previously unknown variety offered for sale, or seen and admired in someone else's garden,

HARDY
•◦ PERENNIALS ◦•

The large majority of hardy perennials came to us as a result of the expeditions undertaken by the Plant Hunters. From the sixteenth century onwards, these brave men have faced deprivations and danger; some have even died in their search for the diverse range of plants which now adorn our gardens.

One of their benefits is that they are supposed to be able to grow in the open air all the year and last several years. Herbaceous perennials die down annually but regrow each spring. Some, as their common names may indicate, have short-lived blooms, for example, the Day Lily has flowers that open and fade in one day, others bloom for weeks and many subsequently produce seedheads or coloured leaves that enhance the border until late autumn. Their colours range through the whole spectrum, their heights from a modest few inches to giants of over eight feet, with an infinite range of form and foliage.

that all may not be as it seems. A little time spent in research may save you a great deal of disappointment and aggravation later on. To buy plants that are suitable for your low-maintenance borders it is as important to learn how to interpret the glowing descriptions, so temptingly illustrated in plant catalogues, as it is to make sure you buy from a reputable firm, who will supply healthy plants with well-established roots. With experience you will learn to translate some of the euphemisms contained in these publications (see *Plant Terminology*).

Armed with this knowledge and having made your own investigations when visiting other gardens, and above all having picked the brains of your most expert friends, you can safely proceed to making your choice.

PLANT HABITS AND HARDINESS

Plant habits vary in different areas. In the north-east of Scotland where I live, the long hours of daylight from spring to autumn and the almost perfect soil with which we are blessed mean the majority of plants grow very vigorously. My first summer here I grew standard-sized annuals, and was amazed at the height they attained. Happily a local

Clump-forming plants such as Pearly Everlasting (Anaphalis triplinervis) are recommended for the easy border.

Although sometimes described as groundcover, Brunnera macrophylla is really quite well behaved.

When buying tall plants make sure they are like Echinacea purpurea which, despite reaching up to 1.2m (4ft) high, does not require staking.

◆• PLANT TERMINOLOGY •◆

GROUNDCOVER Almost without exception, a plant that will not only cover ground, but also do it so efficiently that you may end up with a great deal more ground covered than you really wanted. Extremely useful for large areas, they are seldom suitable for the border especially if it is a small one.

STATELY/HANDSOME May describe a tall, in many cases a *very* tall, plant that will need staking and protecting from strong winds.

VIGOROUS Applies to those plants that are capable of doubling in size in a surprisingly short time.

GRACEFUL/ARCHING SPRAYS Will probably mean they need a great deal of support.

SPREADING Should be viewed with extreme caution.

RAPIDLY SPREADING Avoided at all costs in the easy border.

CLUMP FORMING, LOW GROWING, NEAT APPEARANCE, RESTRAINED HABIT OF GROWTH Descriptions to look out for.

resident informed me, in time for the following season, that I should order dwarf varieties, and these duly grew to the size I was accustomed to expect from normal varieties in the south.

There is a line in a well-known hymn, which enjoins the ocean 'it's own appointed limits keep' and I frequently wish my plants would heed this exhortation! Of course, height and spread, and the plant's ability to survive, depend on the conditions prevailing in your garden. Factors to be taken in account are shown in the box (right).

SOIL

Types of soil vary tremendously; they may be alkaline or acid, and contain varying amounts of clay or sand, flints, stones and gravel. Most hardy perennials are tolerant of a wide range of soils, but details of specific requirements are given under each entry in the Plant Directories.

CLAY SOIL is described as heavy. It is sticky when wet, hard when dry, and is slow to warm up in spring. Use organic matter to improve it.

SANDY SOIL is described as light; water drains rapidly from it, as do nutrients and it warms up quickly in spring. Improve it with organic matter.

SILTY SOIL is sticky and fairly heavy but it can be improved with the addition of humus-producing materials.

LOAM is the ideal soil, containing a mixture of clay, sand and silt, and having adequate nutrients.

⟝• YOUR GARDEN'S CLIMATE •⟞

For true success in gardening it is vital to be thoroughly familiar with the conditions prevalent in your garden. Take into account the following:
TYPE OF SOIL   and the amount of humus and fertiliser it contains.
WEATHER   the average rainfall, hours of daylight and sunshine normally expected and how cold it gets in winter.
PREVAILING WIND   and how sheltered your garden is. (Walled gardens are reputed to enjoy temperatures up to 5°C (10°F) higher than the average, more exposed ones.) trees and hedges produce not only shelter, but shade; salt-laden winds will limit the range of plants you can grow. Finally your skill as a gardener will also affect the performance of your plants.

WEATHER

Very cold winters, with exceptional levels of frost and snow, are hazards most of us have to face from time to time. However, most of the perennials listed in the Plant Directory have survived some exceptionally bitter weather in my garden. Some years ago the temperature fell to around −26°C (−15°F) in this area, but very few of my perennials perished; the main victims were shrubs, killed by the intense cold and the weight of snow, which split the central branches. Those plants that may require some protection are clearly indicated (see General Cultivation, p28, for details of how best to prepare your beds and borders for the winter).

Areas of frost can vary within a few hundred yards in some areas. Frost 'pockets', into which the cold permeates, are likely to damage plants that produce early shoots and blooms so be careful where

TESTING YOUR
⟝• SOIL •⟞

Simple soil-testing kits allow you to check whether your soil is acid or alkaline. Best results are obtained by taking samples from several parts of the garden.

⟝• FROST POCKETS •⟞

Valleys and areas at the bottom of slopes are most susceptible to frost because cold air, like water, flows to the lowest level. Hedges or solid fences act as traps and cold air will collect in front of them. Less dense barriers may help to alleviate this problem.

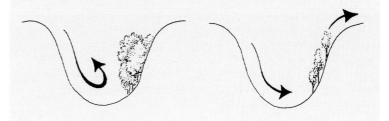

you site them. Late frosts can affect the emerging shoots of some perennials, but in most cases this will merely check the plant's growth, and not do irreparable harm.

Rainfall and sunshine are factors over which none of us have control, but we can certainly take measures to alleviate the effects of either too much, or too little, of the former (see General Cultivation, (p28)).

WIND

We are fortunate in that a wild cherry wood protects us from the prevailing south-west wind, but the first time it went round to the east, we very quickly realised why the previous owners planted that tall laurel hedge we had been so anxious to remove. Needless to say, it remains, although trimming it is a yearly chore that no one enjoys.

In the easy border, wind should not adversely affect the plants to any great extent, but gales can wreck the best planned garden and bring heartbreak to its owner. If there is one thing the dedicated gardener requires in full measure it is resilience; the capacity to accept, albeit reluctantly, the set-backs and disasters that will inevitably occur.

PLANT AVAILABILITY

With the growth of interest in perennial plants has come a comparable increase in the number of garden centres that stock them; there has also been a vast improvement in the range on sale. Even more exciting is the attendant proliferation of small, specialist nurseries, which offer the more unusual and desirable plants that were so often previously unobtainable. The temptation these last present is well-nigh irresistible and you will soon discover how addictive the less well known perennials can become, especially if you develop a fondness for a certain genus or species and wish to build up a collection of its varieties and cultivars.

There is also a whole range of plant societies, each devoted to a particular speciality or plant. Membership will bring not only a wealth of information, advice and guidance, but also the opportunity to participate in seed distribution schemes and exchange of plants services. It can bring, too, the opportunity to make a great many new friends, all sharing the same enthusiasm, and the chance to visit some gardens not normally open to the general public. In Britain the so-called National Collections sponsored by the National Council for the Conservation of Plants and Gardens, now number over five hundred. These are safe havens for many endangered plants and can provide, when needed, the necessary material for cross-breeding and the development of new cultivars.

Thanks to the efforts of all these societies, many of the rarer varieties are traced and propagated and some perhaps thought to have been lost are once more available and safe for future generations. The dedicated members and staff deserve our support and gratitude, for they are building the Noah's Ark of the modern world, rescuing and saving for the future many plants that would otherwise have been lost forever.

Local plant sales can produce a wealth of seedlings, off-sets and cuttings, and are particularly useful for those with a limited budget. However, do remember my previous warning, and find out all you can of

•◦ NEW ACQUISITIONS ◦•

If in any doubt as to the behaviour of plants you have been given or have been unable to resist at the sales, do not plant them until you can check their credentials. If they are well rooted and established plants, they will come to no harm left in their containers – out of bright sun and well watered – until you have decided where to put them and, indeed, if you really want them.

Bear in mind the golden rule: is it being offered because its owner has too much of the parent plant, or is it, as happily so often happens, a real gem, which someone has taken the trouble to propagate and pass on in the generous spirit of the true plant lover?

your prospective purchase before handing over your money (see *New Aquisitions* box).

Friends, acquaintances, sometimes even total strangers, who share a love of plants will prove the most generous of benefactors. Over the years I have been given a wealth of plants and although

plants. I often think of it as being comparable to an archeologist unearthing some ancient and long buried object, or an art collector finding a vanished masterpiece to add to his collection. The sense of achievement and satisfaction these unexpected finds provide is tremendously rewarding.

Well run nurseries have well maintained and healthy plants, and it pays to seek them out. Reputable firms who run mail order services will send you plants that are properly packed and well rooted. They have their reputations to uphold and usually guarantee their orders, although not, of course, against losses incurred by your own mismanagement or exceptionally bad weather in their first season. Order early, especially if you are after any new or improved variety as these can become 'unavailable' all too quickly. Well known firms have become 'well known' as a result of the quality and range of plants they offer. Many send out, either once or twice a year, beautifully illustrated catalogues full of plants that are very hard to resist.

Many perennials can also be raised easily and cheaply from seed and I have given details of how to do this in the section on propagation (p.28).

many proved to be too rampant for my taste, I have also received among them a selection of some of the most delectable and sought after plants, such as old varieties of dianthus or double primroses. On one occasion I was given a variety of *Echinops* that, years later, I discovered was on the rare and endangered 'pink' list of the National Council for the Conservation of Plants and Gardens. The donor had been given a root by his mother, and neither they, nor I, had any idea how valuable it was until I sent a specimen to a botanic garden for identification.

It is this constant exchange of material that so often ensures the survival of

---

◆• WHAT TO LOOK FOR WHEN BUYING A PLANT •◆

You can tell a lot about a garden centre or nursery from its overall appearance and the state of the plants it has to offer.

WEEDS as well as plants, in the containers and wilting and bedraggled specimens will warn you that their condition is not all it should be.

ROOTS growing out of the base of the pot indicate that the plant has been in that container too long and should have been potted-on; its roots will be congested and it will have been checked in its growth; it will also suffer a further set-back if the roots are torn when you try to remove it from the container and it will take longer to establish itself in its new surroundings.

BROWNING AND SHRIVELLING OF THE LEAVES of containerised plants usually denotes lack of water and/or feeding, frost damage and possibly even disease.

Avoid specimens with any or all of these problems when making your selection.

DESIGN

My garden was, and is still, a cottage garden. We have retained the original design in front of the house – herbaceous borders on either side of the main path and the areas beside these for growing our fruit and vegetables. We bought the property some years before we could live there full time and during this period could only work on the garden on our all too infrequent visits. Consequently, plants tended to be put in place in a rather unplanned fashion. However, this is the way most cottage gardens developed, and we wanted ours to retain its original form and complement the carefully restored cottage. Most of the 'But and Ben' cottages in this area (traditional two-roomed, Scottish dwellings) have been modernised so drastically that, not only have all traces of their original character and charm vanished, but the old gardens have disappeared as well. Our aim was to restore the cottage and garden so that there would be, in this area at least, one example of the local style.

As my own preference is for cottage gardens, and this book is primarily about choosing plants, I am not going to advise you on design in any great detail. (There are many excellent books on the subject written by a host of experts who can guide and enlighten you. I would not dream of treading on their toes with my own somewhat liberal views.) However, there are some points that I think may be helpful and which you may like to consider. I have already listed the main factors to take into account, such as situation, soil, and local weather conditions, but perhaps the most important aspect is suitability, not only of the plants you choose, but also of the type of garden you are going to create. Ask yourself: Are the plants suitable for my garden, and is my garden 'right' for my house?

Suburban and town gardens have their own merits and disadvantages, but should look like town gardens, and contain

One of the traditional herbaceous borders at House of Pitmuies, Angus, Scotland, with a colour scheme of blue, yellow and white flowers. The tall plants are supported by strong nets which run the length of the border, set in place early in spring at an angle of 30 degrees, they are soon hidden by the foliage. This method of support does away with the need to stake individual plants or clumps; in a long border this would be time-consuming and tedious. Hand-weeding is only possible at the front of the border and a weed glove is used to treat any couch grass or tall weeds that grow through the nets.

plants that are suited to these environs. Conversely, overly neat bedding schemes of annuals, flanked by elaborate patios and tidy conifers, simply do not go in small, informal country gardens, neither do immaculately kept lawns. All these can look well in large, formal gardens in both town and country, but if you live in a cottage it is more natural, and pleasing, to have a garden that matches it. The choice is, of course, wholly dependent on what you want and on your own ideas of what is right. Part of the charm of many gardens lies in the idiosyncratic taste of their owners and it would be a dull world indeed if we all had similar ones. However, a little sympathetic understanding of the style and age of your house, and its setting, never goes amiss when planning the garden.

HOW TO START

For both old and new gardens, the advice is the same: do not be in too much of a hurry, get to know your garden before you start rearranging it. Take time to plan and ponder, it will almost certainly pay dividends in the future.

If you are laying out a new garden you will be able to position your trees, shrubs, beds and borders as you please. Those of us who have had to accept the basic plantings of previous owners are limited in what we can do by existing layouts. Obviously trees and shrubs can be cut down, and paths and beds relocated, but it is usually preferable to keep as much of the original design as is possible and to limit any large scale rearrangements to the minimum. Judicious pruning and lopping of overgrown branches can sometimes avoid the necessity of removing a tree completely (see *Established Gardens* box).

COLOUR SCHEMES

Not everyone would agree, but over the years I have found, with a few exceptions, the truth of the saying, 'No colours clash in nature'. There is something about the luminosity of flower petals and the texture of leaves, that allows a whole spectrum of colours to live quite harmoniously side by side, colours that in any other situation would not be acceptable. My husband, who is an amateur artist, frequently draws my attention to the glorious shade of green that appears each spring with the emerging leaves and new grass. He points out that when they are reproduced with paint on paper the result, though quite exact, produces the most disgusting colour imaginable!

Anyone anxious to have colour co-ordinated flower beds and borders would do well to read Gertrude Jekyll's *Colour Schemes for the Flower Garden*, which is considered to be the definitive work on the subject.

Trollius and doronicum flower in the spring and make perfect companions in the early border

---

⚬• ESTABLISHED GARDENS •⚬

If you are taking over an established garden, it is always wise to take time before embarking on any major changes; it is advisable to wait and see what plants appear in their due season before deciding which to remove or reposition. There may well be some pleasant surprises. We certainly had no idea of the number of bulbs our garden contained and were enchanted when a whole range of daffodils, some of them old varieties, appeared in the spring.

Serendipity oftens springs pleasant and unexpected delights. Even with my over-hasty and random original planting, I had some delightful surprises. Yellow dor-onicum, one of the survivors of the old borders, made a surprise appearance in the spring alongside a clump of yellow trollius, given to me by one of the village's oldest inhabitants. The flowers not only bloom at the same time, but complement each other perfectly, and their placing was purely accidental. Like garden design, there are innumerable books on the subject of garden colour schemes and complementary planting, so I don't intend to go into much detail here.

Unless you are extremely well orga-nised and know exactly the effect you wish to achieve as regards shape, form and colour, you must expect to make

mistakes. These can be put right (see *Rectifying Mistakes* box) and you will learn a lot in the process. The best gardens have evolved over many years, with constant changes and innovations. Read, research, observe and take advice, but in the end it is your garden, and if you like it that is all that matters. Leave the cognoscenti to argue the finer points of garden design and colour and just enjoy your own.

●• RECTIFYING MISTAKES •●

As far as both designs and colour schemes are concerned, a word of warning, applicable to both the plant and its placing: Remember that you will have to wait until the autumn if you wish to rectify any mistakes. A perennial does not take kindly to being moved in midsummer, so you will have to put up with it where it is, until it has died down in the autumn and can be safely repositioned.

A well designed, mixed border with a pleasing colour scheme of blue and pink aquilegias, tulips and Dutch irises. Ajuga reptans in the foreground is a 'groundcover' plant which will quickly become invasive, and is therefore not suitable for the easy border. Suitable alternative plants include Veronica gentianoides and Brunnera macrophylla.

PATHS, WALLS AND HEDGES

PATHS

Paths need careful thought if you are designing a new garden. Bear in mind not only the amount of traffic they will have to contend with, but also the maintenance they will require (see *What Type of Path?* box).

If you decide on a grass path the choice between turf or seed depends on how quickly you want results, and what you can afford. Turf is hideously expensive, but instantaneous; seeding is much quicker than one would imagine. It is very important, in any case, to choose a suitable grass, such as perennial rye grass mixture, which will withstand the wear and tear of both feet and machinery. Our

◦• WHAT TYPE OF PATH? •◦

GRAVEL   is available in a good range of both size and colour. Although it is no longer cheap, it is relatively long lasting. Weeds do seed themselves in it, but they can be safely controlled with modern herbicides, which, although they are expensive, do cut down the tiresome job of weeding. My only objections to gravel are that wheelbarrows are difficult to push over it and it can be unpleasant to walk on, especially for people who are unstable on their feet.

PAVING STONES   especially old ones if you are lucky enough to find them, are excellent, as long as they are really well laid and level. Weeds will grow between them, but can be removed either by using an old blunt knife or by resorting to weed killers.

GRASS PATHS   are lovely alongside borders, but they can make a lot of work with the inevitable trimming and mowing. In frosty, or very wet, weather grass paths are easily damaged by heavy boots and wheelbarrows; after a heavy frost it is essential to wait until the grass has thawed out before walking on it. Bad weather at any time of the year can be very trying, especially when it prevents you from walking on, and working from, grass paths. Plants may flop over making trimming the edges tricky; they often also create bald patches, which look unsightly when the plant is cut back.

BRICKS   old ones in particular, are not a wise choice for paths; they can break up in frosty weather and make an uneven surface on which to walk or push wheelbarrows.

A combination of paving stones and grass makes the ideal solution. My central path is paved, those behind the borders are grass. I can always reach the plants as the design of the borders means they are accessible from either the back or the front.

Random paving

Paving slabs

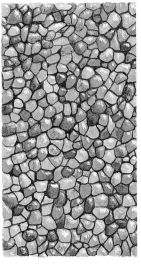

Coarse gravel

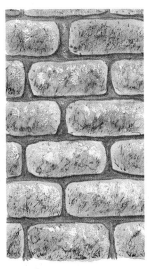

Granite setts

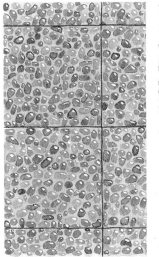

Pebbled flagstones

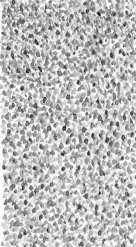

Fine gravel

original paths were so full of couch grass and weeds, that eventually we gave up the unequal struggle and lifted them. The ground was dug and carefully weeded, levelled, firmed and seeded. To our amazement the new paths were ready for mowing in about six weeks. The cost was minimal and the results have been excellent.

To ensure that border and path keep themselves apart, we have placed edging stones at their meeting point. These are of a composite material and, having been painted with a mixture of diluted manure, are now weathering down well, and will soon lose their new appearance. There is a good range of edging stones available. Ours are 20cm (8in) deep and have been sunk into the soil, so that only 5-8cm (2-3in) remain above ground.

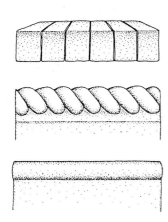

An aid to easy gardening is to position some 'stepping stones' at various places in the border itself (see *Stepping Stones* box).

You may be lucky enough to have, or be able to obtain, those old round 'staddle' stones, that were used to prevent rats climbing into barns, but composite ones are quite acceptable. There is now a good range of stones, of all shapes and sizes, available in garden centres, and the quality and colour of these is improving all the time.

HEDGES AND WALLS
Hedges and walls provide shelter; they

⊷• STEPPING STONES •⊷

• If you have large, round or oval beds, a careful placing of some of these stepping stones will enable you to reach all the plants without having to stand on the soil. The less you can do this the better as the soil becomes compacted, particularly in wet weather or if your soil is of a heavy, clay composition.

also give shade, which can be a mixed blessing. Tall plants set against them at the back of the border will tend to lean forward towards the light and grow even taller. In the easy border this should be avoided as much as possible, so allow plenty of space between wall and plant when setting out the latter. Obviously if your border is backed by a hedge you will need this space so you can reach it when it needs clipping (see *Hedges versus Walls* box).

⊷• HEDGES VERSUS WALLS •⊷

HEDGES
• Require regular pruning
• Compete with plants for food and water
• Natural backdrop for plants
• Provide shade and shelter
• Nesting sites for birds and wildlife.

WALLS
• Maintenance free
• Create dry areas in their shelter
• Complementary to many plants
• Provide shade and shelter
• Can be a sterile environment or a refuge for pests such as snails.

<u>LIGHT</u>   Most perennials like full sun, (although some will tolerate partial shade).

<u>TREES</u>   will not only shade the bed, but the fallen leaves will make extra work in the autumn.

<u>ROOTS</u>   of trees and hedges will compete with the plants for food and water.

BEDS AND BORDERS

SITING AND PREPARING

The size and shape of your bed or border will depend on where it is to be placed and what effect you wish to create.

The 'traditional herbaceous border is

usually long and narrow and is often backed by a hedge or a wall. Double borders are divided by a central path of either grass or paving. The border can be as wide or narrow as you wish, but if you want easy access to the plants, keep them to a manageable width. My original borders were too wide for me to weed the middle from either the back or the front and required tortuous manoeuvering among the plants to reach this inaccessible area. They have now been narrowed, so I can reach the centre from either side, and this has made weeding and staking much easier. Stepping stones are useful, placed at several intervals (see Paths p.18). In a wide border, or a free-standing bed, they are particularly helpful, as you can stand on them, rather than the soil, when gardening and you are less likely to step on neighbouring plants.

LAYING OUT BORDERS

Having decided on the length and width of the border, work it out using either string and bamboo poles or, better still, lengths of wood cut to the correct width of the new border. Lay these in position on the soil, or grass, to guide you (see also *Laying Out Free-Standing Beds* box).

DIGGING

If you are laying out a new bed and are lucky enough to have good soil, it will be sufficient preparation to dig the bed, carefully removing all weeds, and adding

◦• LAYING OUT FREE-STANDING BEDS •◦

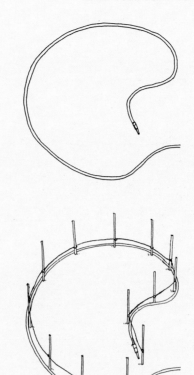

A bed set in a lawn can be any size or shape you like and a good way of marking it out is by using a hose pipe.
• Lay the hose pipe on the ground in the shape of your chosen design; any changes to the original plan are easily made by repositioning
• When you have decided on the final shape, position some short bamboos or sticks at intervals around the hose, then link them by tying strong string or twine between them
• Remove the hose and dig the bed
• If you are cutting out the bed from a lawn, protect the grass by laying down a large sheet of heavy duty polythene, on to which you can place the turf and soil you are removing.

G7868

plenty of well-rotted manure or compost. If you have heavy clay soil with poor drainage, double digging will repay your efforts by giving the plants the best possible foundation on which to grow (see *Double Digging* box).

A new bed needs to be left for several weeks to allow the soil to settle, and is

(opposite) *Nora Craig's lovely garden at Dunnichen, Angus, Scotland. The old wall gives shelter and warmth as well as providing an attractive background for the perennials, old roses and some climbing plants.*

◦• DOUBLE DIGGING •◦

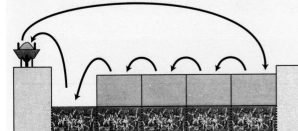

• Take out the first spit, A, and put it at the other end of the border or bed
• Break up the sub-soil

using a strong fork and remove any large stones – small ones help drainage
• Add plenty of well-rotted manure or leaf mould and work this in well
• Turn the adjoining spit, B, on to A, add compost, damp peat or coir, and incorporate this into the soil, also scooping in a handful of bonemeal

• Proceed in this way, carefully removing any weeds and taking special care with those that have long tap roots, such as dandelion, dock or bindweed. Any broken portions of these weed roots left in the soil will regrow, so time taken now, ensuring you get the whole of the weed out, will pay dividends in the future.

LIMERICK COUNTY LIBRARY

best prepared in the autumn, as frost will help to break down heavy clumps and make planting easier in the spring.

If you are rejuvenating or enlarging an existing bed, it is advisable to lift any surviving plants. This will not only enable you to check the roots for weeds, but also allow you to replant them in clean, enriched soil. Some clumps may also need dividing before replacing them in the bed.

All this may sound like a lot of hard work, and it is, but taking short cuts can have disastrous consequences, as I know to my cost. When I started restoring my old borders I did not realise to what extent they were infested with couch grass and, in my ignorance, I left some surviving clumps untouched. I gave strict instructions to the kindly villager who was helping us in the garden, that in our absence he was *not* to touch the herbaceous borders. When we returned some months later, I found they had been freshly dug and all traces of the surviving plants had vanished. Alarmed at the number of weeds emerging, he had thought it best to dig the beds, and had done this by merely turning over the soil as he would a vegetable patch. Needless to

⊸• PLANTING •⊶

BARE-ROOTED PLANTS
• Soak well with water and cut off any roots that are dead, or look unhealthy

• Make up a planting mixture in a wheelbarrow or bucket. This can be a combination of garden soil, damp peat and well-rotted compost or manure

• Put some of the mixture into the hole, then set the plant in position
• Add planting mixture as you go, making sure it falls around the roots by gently shaking the plant
• Ensure the base of the stem is at the same level in the soil that it was before the plant was lifted. It is

usually possible to see where this was if you look carefully

• Firm the plant gently, and water well, using a watering can with a rose so as not to swamp the soil.

CONTAINERISED PLANTS
• Soak well if the compost is not already sufficiently moist

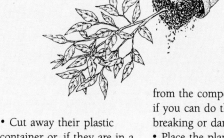

• Cut away their plastic container or, if they are in a pot, turn them upside down, and tap the base smartly, allowing the root ball to ease out gently

• If the roots are very congested, try easing some of the larger ones away

from the compost, but only if you can do this without breaking or damaging them
• Place the plant in the hole as described in planting bare-rooted plants, filling in around the sides with planting mixture
• Make sure the top of the root ball is about an inch below the surface of the soil
• Firm the plant in gently and water.

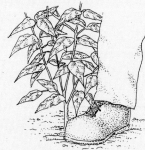

say, most of the couch grass had been dug in along with the soft weeds. When I exclaimed in horror, 'You have dug up all my plants', I got the immortal reply, 'I hae na dug em oop, missus, I dug em doon', and so he had! For several years, portions of the survivors would struggle to the surface, along with copious amounts of couch grass, and I learnt how vital it is to ensure that preparatory work is carefully done at the beginning.

PLANTING

Plants in containers can be planted out at any time of the year, although obviously not when the ground is frosted or extremely wet. Bare-rooted ones can be planted in either spring or autumn. In colder areas I recommend waiting until spring, when the plants have a better chance of establishing themselves. It is the time of reawakening and natural growth for perennials and they will respond accordingly. Put in place in the autumn in cold areas, they may have to contend with very harsh conditions – the roots may rot or be killed by frost – and they may not survive the winter. In milder areas, where the soil will still be warm, they have a better chance of getting established before the bad weather arrives, and can be planted in the autumn.

It is important, when planting, to ensure that the hole is large enough to accommodate the roots (see *Planting* box).

COMPOST AND FERTILISERS

COMPOST

Plants require food and water, as well as sunshine and warmth, to grow. Perennials planted in good soil with plenty of humus will withstand drought conditions when those in poor soil will suffer. Providing humus can be a problem in a new garden that has not had time to make a good supply of compost (see *Compost Heap* box). It is usually possible

•· COMPOST HEAP ·•

Put a compost heap at the top of your priority list if you are starting a new garden. There is a wide range of compost bins on the market, although most are only large enough for very small gardens. It is not difficult to make your own using strong posts and planks. Slot in the front planks so you can lift them off as you work down the heap and remove the compost more easily. A sheet of strong wire mesh, supported by bricks, placed at the base of the heap will allow air into the compost and help increase heat, which will speed up the rotting of the material and help to kill off weed seeds. (See diagram.) Occasional applications of a proprietary activator will also speed up the process.

Two bins are ideal – one ready for use and the other rotting down. This will save having to lift off the unrotted, top layer, when you want to reach the compost that is ready for use at the bottom.

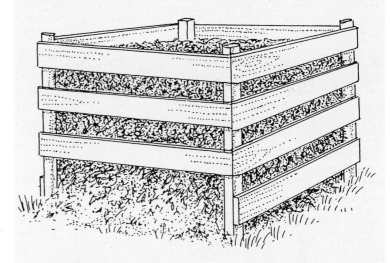

WHAT TO PUT IN
- Soft weeds that have not set seed
- Small amounts of grass cuttings
- Vegetable and fruit waste from the kitchen.

WHAT NOT TO PUT IN
- Weeds with tap roots, such as dandelion, dock, elder and bindweed, as these will regrow
- Large amounts of grass cuttings as these become compacted
- Leaves – they are best rotted down separately (see *Leaf Mould* box)
- Thick, woody stems which will not rot down easily
- Cooked food – it will attract vermin, and smells.

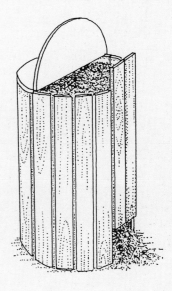

•● *LEAF MOULD* ●•

Leaf mould also makes valuable humus, and is ideal for use with miniature azaleas, rhododendrons and primroses. A container for leaves can be made using strong wire netting, or you can put the leaves into old plastic sacks. Fill the bags with leaves, tie the top and make a few holes in it using the prongs of a fork. Either type of container can be stacked in a corner of the garden, or behind a shed, and the leaf mould will be ready for use in about a year. Use soft leaves, such as beech, chestnut and oak, not evergreen ones, as these will not rot down successfully.

to find a local supplier of manure – riding stables and farms – but make sure it is well rotted, as fresh manure will burn the roots of plants, as well as being malodorous! Spent mushroom compost, if available, or chicken manure, is also suitable, and it is possible to buy soil improvers from garden centres, although these tend to be expensive. Damp peat and coir can be used to provide bulk but not food value to the soil.

Bark mulch is available in coarse, medium and fine grades; I find the latter is best for borders, as it does not blow about in windy weather and looks 'natural'. The coarse and medium grades can be used in shrubberies. Coconut chippings are becoming a very popular mulch in the medium to fine range.

A 4cm (2in) mulch will not only conserve moisture, but also greatly reduce the number of weeds. Any that do appear will be easy to pull out.

It is rather expensive, but if you set the cost against the time involved in weeding bare soil it will seem money well spent. If you are paying for help in the garden it is certainly worthwhile, allowing time to be spent on more important work instead of routine cleaning of beds.

FERTILISER

Fertiliser can be either in the form of well-balanced general-purpose granules or bonemeal, which is slow acting, or blood, fish and bone. Organic fertilisers made from natural ingredients such as seaweed are also available. An inexpensive way of giving fertiliser is by foliar feeding. This can be applied using a watering can and a soluble powder, but it is a rather laborious business if you have a large number of plants to feed. It is possible to buy a hosepipe fitting, in which the foliar feed is placed and released at the correct strength along with the water. This is an excellent method if you have a large area to deal with.

WATERING

Even plants set in soil containing plenty of humus and a top mulch will need watering in very dry spells. A hose and sprinkler is the easiest and quickest method. They can be moved so that all parts of the border or bed get their fair share of the water and the joy of a sprinkler is that it will get on with the watering, leaving you free to attend to other jobs in the garden. Sprinklers are very reasonable in price, and there are various models from which to choose, some of which oscillate so watering large areas and reducing the number of times you have to move them. A hose with a hand-held trigger fitting allows you to concentrate water on those plants that need it most, but this method, of course, involves you in its operation. For very small beds, watering cans may be adequate, but if you have to carry more than a few of these it quickly becomes heavy and tiring work.

(opposite) Campanula lactiflora 'Loddon Anna' – one of the 'borderline' plants that are suitable for the back of the border. It may require some support, but is otherwise an easy plant.

(above) Veronica spicata 'Red Fox', a charming, neat-growing perennial, suitable for the front of the border. Coarse gravel has been used here as a weed-suppressing mulch.

PETS, PESTS
DISEASES AND WEEDS

At one time we kept cats and they proved to be less than compatible with an easy garden. They had a passion for the Catmint (*Nepeta*) and would roll and lie on the plants, which were permanently flattened as a result. Any freshly dug soil provided them with a chance to dig holes and perform their bodily functions, with disastrous consequences to newly planted seed beds and seedlings. Sadly, they were not good news for the birds either, although in their favour they did keep down damage by mice and pigeons. Much as we loved the cats, we find life much easier without their presence in the garden.

We also kept ducks on the stream, and even these enchanting creatures were not averse to grubbing in flower beds. On one occasion they ate a number of containerised herbs that I had left out prior to taking them to a friend. This led to some rather unkind remarks being made, by other members of the family, about the advisability of herb-fed roast duck on the weekend menu. Duck exclusion zones were created with a wire netting fence. Sadly, some years later, the local fox ensured that duck damage was no longer a problem.

Pigeons can be a general nuisance in a garden, but should not be a problem in the border. Slugs and snails, however, can

Groundsel

be, and you will have to watch out for damage to emerging shoots of perennials in the spring, especially if you live in an area where these pests are a particular problem (see *Combating Slugs* box).

How you control pests and diseases will depend on whether you are an organic or inorganic gardener. Passions run high on this subject and I do not wish to take sides in the argument, but I feel sure that we all wish to keep the use of harmful pesticides to the absolute minimum. A solution of soft soap and water is often effective against aphids, and birds, such as warblers and blue tits, definitely reduce the number of these pests in the garden.

If you choose to use an insecticide the most important thing to remember is always to spray late in the afternoon or in the early evening, when the bees and birds are no longer feeding on the flowers. Both pests and diseases should be minimal in your easy border, as those plants that are very prone to attack are, for the most part, excluded from the Plant Directories. Details of any that may be susceptible are given under the relevant entry.

WEED CONTROL

The word 'weeds' comes from the Anglo-Saxon 'woeds', meaning small plants and herbs. Many were used as food; Fat hen, (*Chenopodium album*), which can produce ½ million seeds from one plant, was eaten before spinach became available, as were the tips of nettles. There is a saying 'When the weeds begin to grow is the time to sow', and this does seem to hold true,

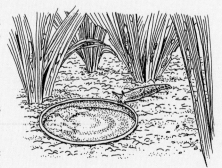

•• *COMBATING SLUGS* ••

• Sprinkle slug pellets around the plants. Choose a brand that is not harmful to birds, dogs or children
• Buy slug traps, or make your own. Jars half filled with beer and set into the soil beside vulnerable plants can be effective, as can a circle of soot, or coarse gravel, sprinkled around the base of the plant.

Fat Hen

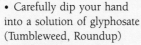

Weed gloves are the best way to remove steadfast weeds from in and around clumps of perennials.
• Put an old cotton or woollen glove over the heaviest rubber glove you can buy

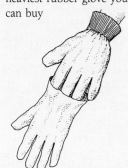

• Carefully dip your hand into a solution of glyphosate (Tumbleweed, Roundup)
• Squeeze hard to remove

any excess mixture, and then stroke the couch grass or weed with the glove
• Make sure the stroked weed does not touch any nearby plants. The effects, although taking some time to become apparent, are excellent; the weed absorbs the mixture which is carried down to its roots and ultimately it dies.

This is a much easier and quicker way of getting rid of perennial weeds than lifting and dividing the clumps in autumn or spring.

Shepherd's purse

however, it is as well to remember that some weeds, Chickweed, Groundsel and Shepherd's Purse, can set seed in every month of the year.

Weed control will depend on your chosen method of dealing with the problem. A top mulch of shredded bark (p.25) is the best way to avoid unnecessary weeding, but, of course, will not completely eliminate it. Even if the soil has been cleared of weeds before planting, some portions of tap-rooted weeds may remain and these will regrow. This regeneration is thought to be a defence mechanism to counteract grazing by cattle. Soft weeds are easily removed, but it is not easy to trace and dig up the roots of couch grass and underground elder, especially if, as so often happens, they are in the middle of a clump of perennials. The best way to deal with these is by using a 'weed glove' (see *Weed Glove* box).

If you have not applied a top mulch, you can kill weeds using a watering can containing a glyphosate solution and fitted with a trickle bar. (Clearly label the watering can 'Weedkiller' to avoid accidental use.) This method allows you to get within a few inches of the plants, but care is needed, especially in the spring, when

new shoots may still be emerging from the soil. This method is also useful for weeding paved areas, but be sure none of the mixture runs off on to plants. Glyphosate is inactivated as soon as it touches the earth and is, therefore, a very safe weed killer. New plants can be set out in the treated area almost immediately.

Bindweed is particularly difficult to eradicate, which is hardly surprising considering the roots are reputed to be able to reach depths of 8m (25ft). The best method is as follows:
• Pour a small amount of weedkiller into a jar with a screw-top lid
• Carefully unwind the bindweed tendrils and lay them down on the soil or a path (if it is not a grass one)
• Using a one-inch paint brush

apply weedkiller
• Always replace the jar lid as you work so there is no danger of accidental spillage
• Painting other weeds such as dandelion this way is very effective, particularly if done on a hot, sunny day.

GENERAL CULTIVATION

In spring, gardens and gardeners alike 'spring' into life after the slow, quiet winter months. Setting out new plants, lifting and dividing overgrown or old clumps, weeding, feeding, grass cutting and trimming hedges make this the busiest time of the year.

The easy border should require little attention in summer, although watering will be necessary in dry seasons. Weeding will also have to be done regularly if a bark mulch has not been used.

In autumn both plants and gardeners slow down, and clearing and tidying beds and borders can be done at a leisurely pace when time and weather permit.

SPRING

In new beds or borders, you will already have given the plants sufficient fertiliser when setting them out, but in established beds they will welcome a yearly mulch of well-rotted manure or compost, and a handful of bonemeal, or blood, fish and bone, or a general-purpose fertiliser. Make sure the bed is cleared of weeds first. No further feeding should be necessary but if you feel a plant needs a boost, apply foliar feed at any time in the spring and summer. Lay down a top mulch of bark, and maintenance should be minimal for the rest of the season.

AUTUMN

In the autumn, when the perennials have died down, cut out the spent foliage. Put this material on your compost heap for next year's mulch, unless it is very woody or diseased, in which case it is best put on the bonfire. There are a few exceptions to this rule, for instance penstemons, which are tender and welcome the protection given by the spent foliage during the winter months. They are best cut down in the spring. Any plants that you suspect may not enjoy the winter months can be given a mulch of peat or bracken to protect them. Peg down the bracken with pieces of galvanised wire (see left) to prevent it blowing away. Remove any weeds, and then nothing more needs to be done until the following spring.

PROPAGATION AND GROWING FROM SEED

Raising your own perennials from seed is not as difficult as you may imagine. The secret of success often lies in obtaining fresh seed. Those who belong to specialist societies can order from their

◆• SOWING SEED •◆

• Fill a seed tray with potting compost, adding some fine grit or perlite to the mixture to assist drainage
• Sow the seeds thinly and cover them with a fine layer of grit to discourage the growth of algae
• Water the compost
• Place the tray in a cold frame, or corner of the garden. If it is placed outside, you can cover the tray with a piece of glass, but remember to water it from time to time

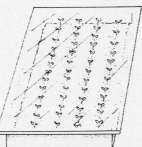

• Once germination has taken place the trays can either be left in the cold frame, or brought into the greenhouse
• When the plants are growing well and are about 5cm (2in) tall, carefully transplant them into 7cm (3in) pots. Most perennials have long roots and will not have sufficient room to grow in a seed tray

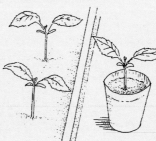

• Place the pots in the cold frame until all danger of frost has passed then place them in a sheltered corner of the garden where the plants will not get scorched by the sun
• Plant those that are large enough in their permanent positions late in the summer. Any you suspect may not withstand the winter can be potted on into larger pots if necessary, and placed back in the cold frame until the following spring.

annual seed list, or obtain them from good seed firms or friends who grow the plants.

Some seed, that of *Eryngiums* for instance, needs to be sown immediately it is ripe for best results. Watch the pods carefully. As soon as the seed will come away from the pod, pick the head, and lay it out in a dish to dry. After a few days you will be able to shake out the seed, which can then be sown. If you need to store it, make sure it is completely dry and put it in an envelope – clearly labelled – and keep it in a dry, cool place.

To grow perennials from seed follow the simple instructions below. You can raise seedlings in a cold frame or outside. In nature the seeds ripen, fall to the ground and are subjected to the weather. Cold breaks their dormancy, and in the spring, with warmth, they germinate. By placing the seed trays outside you are copying nature and giving the seeds the conditions they need to grow. Some seeds can take a very long time to start into growth so do not be in a hurry to throw away any you think may be failures.

CUTTINGS

Increasing plants by taking cuttings is not always easy, but it is well worth trying. *BASAL STEM CUTTINGS* of herbaceous plants that produce clusters of new shoots at the base in spring, such as delphiniums, can be taken in spring. These are put into potting compost in 7cm (3in) pots.

• Keep the cuttings in a greenhouse or cold frame until they are well rooted and growing strongly. It is a sensible precaution to dip or spray the cuttings with fungicide solution before inserting them into the compost.

• Enclosing the pot in a polythene bag will help to conserve moisture and generate heat, but this can also cause the cutting to rot from the damp conditions inside the bag, so keep an eye on them. *SOFTWOOD CUTTINGS* of penstemon and diascia are best taken in late summer.

• This involves removal of short lengths of plant from tops of healthy shoots

Softwood cuttings can be taken whenever suitable shoots are available. Take the cutting near the top of a healthily-growing shoot.

• Put into containers filled with perlite and water

• The cuttings root in 6–8 weeks, and can then be put into 7cm (3in) pots of potting compost and kept in the greenhouse or cold frame for the winter. I find this method excellent.

DIVISION

After 3–4 years some perennials need to be lifted and divided because the clump has grown too large, or the centre is not producing strong growth. Plants such as *Aconitum* do not lose vigour but merely get too large. They are easily divided and most parts can be replanted. 'Lifting and dividing' describes how this is done.

There are a few, such as large hostas, that can be very difficult to lift and divide. Hostas make very solid, hard root balls,

Trim the cuttings to a node and remove the lower leaves. The sections should be about 5–8cm (2–3in) long.

Insert the cuttings into perlite or cuttings compost and cover them with a plastic bag.

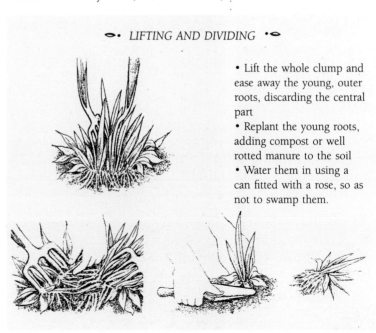

◦• LIFTING AND DIVIDING •◦

• Lift the whole clump and ease away the young, outer roots, discarding the central part

• Replant the young roots, adding compost or well rotted manure to the soil

• Water them in using a can fitted with a rose, so as not to swamp them.

•● ROOT CUTTINGS ●•

• Remove the soil from
around the root
• Cut a length off
• Cut this into short
sections of a few inches.
Make the top of the cut
flat and the bottom
sloping

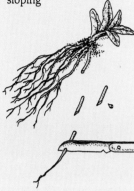

• Insert the sections the
right way up, into pots of
compost with a little
added grit.

and are extremely heavy to dig up. Having
done this you will have to saw the clumps
into sections, making sure there are buds
on each piece, before replanting them.

ROOT CUTTINGS

Plants with long tap roots are very difficult to lift and they may not have any
young offsets that can be removed. The
only way to propagate these, apart from
by seed, is to take root cuttings.

Root cuttings may take some time to
produce growth, but they are usually
successful. They certainly are if you
accidentally leave portions of the root in
the soil when moving such plants as

Eryngium or *Papaver*! I wage perpetual war against some large herbaceous poppies that I was unwise enough to plant in my border many years ago. These pop up every year and the only way I can keep them under control is to treat them with weedkiller. I have never been able to eradicate the root of a Japanese anemone which was in one of the original borders. Despite digging down to extraordinary depths we have obviously never reached the end of the root; each year we apply weedkiller to the leaves, but it still appears and must rate as one of the most persistent and indestructible of all perennial plants.

Midsummer, and the author is at work. I am particularly fond of this plant, Armeria arenaria, which I grew from seed many years ago. Entirely trouble free and one of my 'star performers' it seems to be no longer generally available. I have been unable to find out why this splendid plant and its white form should have disappeared from seed catalogues and nurseries. If you can track it down, or find seed, you will find it a charming plant for the front of the border. Cut off the dead heads after the first flowering is over, and a second flush will appear later in the season. The paved path is extremely hard and the padded kneeler that I am using makes weeding and planting much more comfortable. Turned upside down it makes a stool on which to sit and have a well earned rest!

WORTH NOTING

LABELS

There are two schools of thought on labelling plants. One abhors them, the other welcomes them. While they can detract from the overall appearance of a bed, I have found them essential. Having two large herbaceous borders, it requires a better memory than mine to remember the name of each plant and where it is placed. In the case of a plant that dies down completely, *Incarvillea* for instance, it is all too easy to damage the roots when weeding, before the young shoots have started into growth in the spring. A label to remind you will help avoid this hazard.

Visitors to gardens always want to know which plant they are looking at – novices for information and experts for confirmation that they have identified it correctly. When you have a large number of people all clamouring for names, your memory may tend to play unkind tricks and even a well-known name can refuse to be recalled at the crucial moment. A friend has invented some amusing pseudo-nomenclature for these embarrassing moments. He replies, with all seriousness, 'That is an Oubliata', or (as he lives in Scotland), 'That is a Dinnakenna'. Though these may fool the novice, they do not deceive the expert.

The choice of label depends on two things: what you want and what you can afford.

KEEPING RECORDS

I strongly advise keeping a written record of the plants in your garden. Once a label has been lost you may not be able to remember the name of the plant, and will then be at a loss to know what it is and how to look after it. I have a special record book (these can be bought or you can use an exercise book) and I enter the details of every newly purchased plant in the relevant section, giving its name, when and where it was purchased, and where I have placed it in the garden. It provides a fascinating record of the growth and development of my garden, and is invaluable should a label be lost or my memory fail me. Records of where bulbs are planted are particularly useful, for once the leaves have died down, you have no way of knowing exactly where the bulb is hidden.

SAFETY

The number of gardening accidents recorded each year is proof that not nearly enough care is taken by gardeners. It is surely only sensible to try to reduce the chance of an accident by being aware of inherent dangers and taking all possible precautions against them (see *Safety in the Garden* box).

AIDS TO EASIER GARDENING

Anything that helps to make work easier is always welcome, and there is now a large range of aids available. Kneelers, with padded knee-rests and arm-rests to

---

◦• LABELS •◦

ENGRAVED METAL LABELS used in botanic gardens are ideal, being strong and permanent, but they are also expensive.

PLASTIC LABELS are available in green or white and are very cheap. The name of the plant can be written on them, but they break easily if you tread on them accidentally. Small plastic labels also have a tendency to pop out of the soil in frosty weather.

WOODEN STICKS 30cm (12in) long and 2.5cm (1in) by 1cm (½in) thick are highly recommended. Lengths of suitable wood can be bought and cut to the correct size. Write the plant names using a waterproof pen, crayon, Indian ink or enamel paint. Labels made this way are surprisingly long lasting and are not too conspicuous.

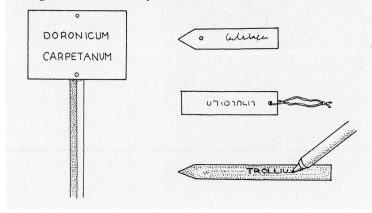

◦• *SAFETY IN THE GARDEN* •◦

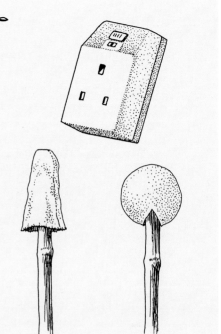

<u>*ELECTRIC MOWERS OR TRIMMERS*</u>   Always use a circuit-breaker plug. It will save your life if you accidentally cut the flex.

<u>*GARDEN TOOLS*</u>   can inflict nasty wounds: rakes should always be propped up, and not left lying on the ground, where they can be stepped on; forks should be stuck into the soil when not in use; and secateurs are safer, as well as being more readily available, when kept in a holster.

<u>*STRONG BOOTS OR SHOES*</u>   with sensible grips on the soles should always be worn. My son once put a sharp fork through his foot. Mercifully, he was wearing rubber boots, but even so he received a deep and painful wound. Paved areas and paths can be slippery in wet or frosty weather, and well-ribbed soles can help prevent falls.

<u>*STICKS AND BAMBOOS*</u>   should always have their tips protected, either by using the special fittings readily available or by using small rubber balls or the fingers cut from old rubber gloves, reinforced with some padding, pushed on to the top of the stick.

<u>*TETANUS*</u>   All gardeners should be aware of the risk of contracting tetanus and should have the full course of preventative injections.

<u>*PESTICIDES AND HERBICIDES*</u>   Sprays of both pesticides and herbicides can be harmful to humans, as well as to insects and weeds, so rubber gloves and face masks should always be used when applying these chemicals.

help one stand up (see photograph on page 31), are excellent for those of us who are not as nimble as we used to be. They can also be up-ended and used as a stool, when a brief rest is required. Knee-pads are a great help; there are several versions on the market.

There is a large selection of tools designed for the disabled, and many of these are excellent for general use. My particular favourite is a long-handled fork, which enables me to reach all sorts of awkward places and is splendid when working among roses, keeping me out of reach of the thorns. Another favourite is my 'humper dumper'. This is a strong, square bag with two handles. It can be used free-standing or inside a wheelbarrow, and, when full, it can be carried or wheeled to the compost heap, and being easily emptied out saves having to fork out the rubbish from the barrow on to the heap. A large, square ground sheet with handles on each corner is excellent for rose or shrub prunings. If the material is laid all in the same direction it can be lifted up and carried, by two people if necessary, to the bonfire.

There are many types of wheelbarrow on the market; one is designed to allow the loading of a sack from ground level, which helps to avoid back injury. We once went on a skiing holiday, and our instructor used to exhort us constantly to 'Bend zee knees' – good advice to remember when lifting heavy loads in the garden.

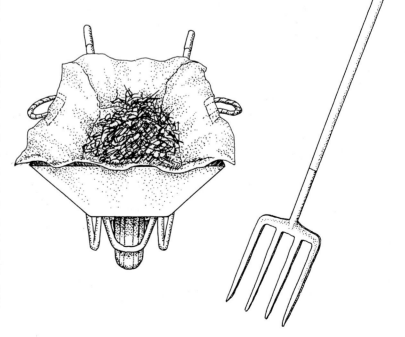

High summer at House of Pitmuies, Angus, Scotland. This is a magnificent example of a pair of traditional herbaceous borders, closely planted with a wide variety of perennials of all colours, forms and heights. The nets that were put in place in early spring have now been completely hidden by foliage and even the tallest varieties are safely supported. This type of border does well in Scotland, and although the plants have to be lifted and divided after some years, the nets and the close planting reduce the amount of work needed in summer. If you want an easy-to-manage garden this type of border is not for you, but in midsummer they provide an unforgettable sight.

HERBACEOUS BORDERS AND MIXED BEDS

HERBACEOUS BORDERS

Before the sixteenth century, when the plant hunters first began making their collecting trips, gardens were primarily for the raising of vegetables, herbs and fruit for food and medicine, although some decorative flowering plants would also have been grown. Over the ensuing centuries, flowering plants increased in popularity and the area allowed for their cultivation was expanded. In larger establishments formal gardens were laid out as 'parterres' of intricate design containing beds of herbs, roses and flowering plants set in grass and surrounded by clipped hedges of box, lavender or other evergreen shrubs. The gardens, or plots of land, belonging to peasants and rural workers continued in much the same way as they had since early times but with the gradual inclusion of more flowers among the herbs and vegetables. Cottagers who worked for large estates were able to obtain cuttings and unwanted plants from the gardens of their employers. These were put in anywhere there was space available, among the vegetables and herbs, which were the most important part of the garden.

BEWARE OF
❖• CONIFERS •❖

Some people favour small conifers, but in my experience these all too frequently exceed the ultimate height and spread forecast for them. They are also very susceptible to lack of water and once they have suffered damage from drought or frost they are almost impossible to prune; the only option is to lift and remove them. As they are expensive to replace, I advise against their inclusion in the easy mixed border, with the possible exception of a few dwarf junipers, which seem better able to cope with adverse conditions than the other kinds of conifer.

(right) *Pale creamy-yellow* Erythronium 'White Beauty' *makes a perfect companion for* Euonymus 'Emerald 'n' Gold *in a mixed border. The marbled leaves of the erythroniums perfectly complement the variegated foliage of the euonymus.*

Herbaceous borders had their heyday in the late nineteenth and early twentieth centuries, when gardeners were not only affordable but in plentiful supply (Miss Willmott had 104). This type of border evolved as the new perennial plants introduced by the plant hunters became more widely available. A large range of plants were set out according to height and colour in long, narrow beds, which were usually backed by a hedge or wall to provide shelter from cold winds. They were either single beds, or two beds separated by a grass path. Although extremely labour intensive, these borders used perennial plants which made it possible to reduce the number of annual plants that had to be raised from seed every year, and set out in beds each spring.

Gertrude Jekyll and William Robinson designed and laid out magnificent gardens and colour co-ordinated herbaceous borders, but the latter gradually fell out of favour. Changed circumstances, brought about by two world wars, and the drastic reduction in both the necessary finance and trained staff, saw their gradual decline. Many were dug up, the plants discarded, to be replaced by grass and shrubs. However, there has been a great resurgence of interest in perennials since the 1950s, in Britain largely due to the Hardy Plant Society, formed in 1957, and the increasingly popular practice of flower arranging.

❖• CHOOSING SHRUBS •❖

The choice of shrubs needs careful thought.
SIZE Make sure you know how tall and wide they will grow and allow for this when planting. Unless you are laying out a large bed, it is essential to choose those that are naturally small and neat growing.
HARDINESS They must be hardy if you live in a cold area.
POSITIONING Bear in mind that shrubs are not as easy to move as perennials if you find you have made a mistake in positioning them, particularly once they are established. Make sure you know how tall and wide they will grow and allow for this when planting.
CHOICE There is a good range available and those listed in the Shrub Directory (p.105) are all easy to maintain and should require little attention beyond an annual feed or mulch and some light pruning.

PAGES 38–39
A lovely border sheltered by a hedge, trees and shrubs, which also provide a background for the flowers, but to the seasoned eye there are several things that make this definitely not an 'easy' border: close planting can make weeding and staking difficult and some of the plants used, for example the artemisia, are very invasive and will soon encroach on their neighbours; other clumps, including the hemerocallis, are very difficult to lift and divide when they outgrow their allotted space.

MIXED BEDS

The mixed bed first came into fashion in the early part of the nineteenth century, when flowering plants and shrubs were both included in the same bed. This kind of planting was later superseded by the herbaceous border, and the formal bedding schemes of annuals fashionable in Victorian and Edwardian times.

Mixed beds or borders have become popular again and can be most attractive, providing the best solution where limited space will not allow separate areas for shrubs and perennials. With one or two exceptions, herbaceous plants die down in the autumn and, once their dead foliage is removed, this leaves an area in the garden devoid of form and colour during the winter months until they start into growth again in the spring. By including shrubs, many of which are evergreen or have variegated foliage, this lack of interest in the bed can be overcome. It also has the advantage of reducing the amount of work involved in maintenance.

The foliage of shrubs provides material for flower arranging and regular cutting helps to keep the shrubs neat and manageable. As an added bonus some, for example, daphne, flower in the winter, many produce berries and deciduous shrubs often have coloured leaves in the autumn and winter.

Roses can be planted in the mixed border, although they are better avoided if you wish to keep maintenance to a minimum. Lovely they undoubtedly are, especially when they do well, but the old shrub roses can grow very vigorously and require pruning. Hybrid tea varieties also require pruning and the removal of dead heads. Spraying against pests and diseases is also usually necessary. All this adds up to a lot of work. Try putting a few miniature roses at the front of a bed, where they can be reached easily. Mine have been successful; pruning them takes only a moment and they seem to be less susceptible to pests and disease than the larger varieties.

Miniature azaleas and rhododendrons can be included. Although these need an acid soil, they will tolerate a mixed bed as long as they are put well away from plants that prefer more lime. The rootballs of miniature azaleas and rhododendrons are very compact, so if you make sure they have a generous amount of damp peat underneath and around them and a top mulch of peat every spring, they usually do well. Mine certainly have. They are delightful plants and a joy in the spring when the perennials are only just starting into growth.

Some varieties of heather, for instance, the *Erica carnea* varieties and the Corsican species *E. terminalis*, will tolerate a limey soil. They can also be included at the front

☞• UNDERSTANDING PLANT NAMES •☜

- Taxonomy is described in my dictionary as 'the science of the classification of living and extinct organisms', and for the novice gardener this science can be a formidable one.
- To illustrate how the system works, take the first plant in the Easy Perennial Directory (p.66). This is *Aconitum*, known also as monkshood, wolf's bane or helmet flower, its common names. Its international name, *Aconitum* is far more specific. The family it belongs to tells us even more. It is Ranunculaceae, quite a large family with *Aconitum* being only one branch, or genus, within it. Other members include *Clematis* and *Aquilegia*.
- Within *Aconitum* there are a number of species, a further division of the genus. The species we have is *Aconitum napellus* which is blue and 1m (3ft) tall.
- If two species are crossed the result is a hybrid. Some species vary naturally, and these are called varieties.
- Those varieties that are deliberately cultivated are known as cultivars. We can set all this information out like this:

> Family: Ranunculaceae
> Genus: *Aconitum*
> Species: *Aconitum napellus*
> Common names: Monkshood, Wolf's Bane & Helmet Flower

- To make things even more difficult the common name Wolf's Bane rightly refers to *A. lycoctonum*, which is a different species.
- Sometimes, for reasons best known to those in charge of plant nomenclature, names are changed, and so you may find the abbreviation syn. after a name. For example *Aconitum carmichaelii* has syn. *A. fischeri*, this being its synonym, or the name by which it was once known.

of the bed or border, as can some of the larger rock garden plants, such as *Aurinia saxatilis* (syn. *Alyssum saxatile*) and *Lithospermum*. These look most attractive spreading out on to a path, though not a grass one where they are likely to cause a bald patch in the grass beneath them.

Bulbs can also be planted in the mixed border, if you do not mind the rather untidy effect of the leaves when they die down. Label their position carefully, as it is all too easy to dig them up accidentally later in the year when weeding or adding a new plant to the bed where you think there is a free space. The Bulb Directory (p.112) includes those that I, and my trusted friends, have found suitable, but the list can be enlarged or contracted according to the area in which you live, and the climate and soil it enjoys – or perhaps suffers from.

TAXONOMY

Latin is the international language of the scientific world and is used universally for the classification of plants. It ensures there is no confusion; a *Calendula* is a *Calendula* all over the world, even though some of us may also call it a Marigold. The trouble with common names is that they tend to be local and vary from one area of a country to another, and may be quite different in another land and language. Charming as they are, common names may not help you when looking for a plant in a catalogue or reference book. In my early days as a gardener I spent fruitless hours searching for Statice, only to find it listed under *Limonium*. Many books give lists of common names with their equivalent botanical names, but even so it is well worth trying to learn and remember the proper names for your plants. Although these appear awesome at first, confidence and understanding will come with practice. There are a few botanical names that even the experts try to avoid, and this does not come as a surprise when you try

SOME MEANINGS

Many of the Latin names are self explanatory.
• *farreri*, *forrestii*, *fortunei*, and *sieboldii* honour the plant hunters Farrer, Forrest, Fortune and Siebold
• *Japonica* tells us the plant comes from Japan
• The colours *albus* (white) *niger* (black) *roseus* (rose-pink) *purpureum* (purple) and *variegata* are all easily understood
• Shapes, textures and sizes may also be used: *spinosus* (spiny), *ovatus* (egg-shaped), and *giganticum* and *obesa*. One of my favourites is *exasperatus*, which is given when the leaves are rough or harsh. *Foetidus* (stinking), *plumosus* (feathery) and *spicatus* (spiky) are also recognisable
I have devised a few names of my own, such as *nuisancei*, *horridus* and *throwoutii*, and no doubt you will do the same.

to get your tongue around twisters such as *Paeonia mlokosewitschii*. Even the stout hearted can be forgiven for choosing the easy way out and referring to 'Molly, the witch'!

Plant classification had its beginnings in the seventeenth century when naturalists began to list plants according to their general appearance into 'families', and then divided the families into more specific 'groups' depending on shared characteristics. These are called genera (plural) or genus (singular). The system that is now universally used was finally organised by Carl Linnaeus, a Swedish naturalist, in the mid-eighteenth century (see *Understanding Plant Names* box).

Once you get used to the latin names it can become quite fun and you will learn a lot about the plants. I was somewhat startled to receive a plant with the inelegant name of *Polygonum superbum;* however, when I had stopped laughing I realised that this was an occasion when correct pronunciation was all important; the stress should be placed on the second syllable!

If you endeavour to use the correct names for your plants, you will find that very soon you will recognise and understand many of the Latin words; familiarity will not breed contempt, but give you confidence.

PAGES 42–43
The pond and famous delphinium border at House of Pitmuies, Angus, Scotland.

Planting Plans

I am a cottage gardener, not a garden designer, so these plans are
meant only as a framework onto which you can impose your own ideas.
They offer a selection of plants that are graded from back to front
according to height and with some attempt at colour co-ordination.

A POOLSIDE PLANTING

Apool is always welcome in a garden: there is nothing quite so relaxing as sitting beside water on a warm summer's day, watching fish swim lazily past and small birds and insects going about their daily business. Just like the borders, there is no need for a pool to be hard work. By making a careful selection of moisture-loving plants you can have an attractive feature without creating any extra labour. Apart from the astilbes and the large hostas, all the plants suggested are from the Directory of Easy Perennials (p.66) and they all prefer moist, but not boggy soil. With luck you should have colour all year round, from the early spring, with the appearance of the hellebores, primulas and dodecatheons in a variety of colours, to the late summer and into autumn, with the pinks of the dierama and the lythrum. This pond is 2–2.5m (6–8ft) long, be prepared to modify your planting around smaller pools and increase it around larger ones.

SMILACINA RACEMOSA likes moist soil and thrives in boggy conditions. It has long lasting flowerheads from late spring to early summer.

ASTILBES need plenty of space and prefer constantly moist soil. With their feathery flowerheads in midsummer they are rewarding to grow.

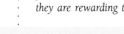

❧• POND MAINTENANCE •❧

Although the plants around the pond are likely to require little attention, the pool itself will need to be looked at carefully.

Problems to consider are:

PREDATORS CATCHING YOUR FISH – including herons and cats. The easiest way to protect the fish is to use wire netting but this is unsightly. Less obvious are strands of fishing wire strung about 25cm (10in) above water level, 15cm (6in) from the edges. A thicket of plants around the pond will discourage cats

WEED GROWTH. All water-growing plants need to be kept under control, including waterlilies, so don't be overzealous in planting. Remove excess growth as soon as it occurs; marginal plants and lilies are best cut back before or after new growth has occurred, in early spring or autumn.

PLANT DEBRIS. It is a good plan to keep the pond as free as possible of falling debris. If you are planning to dig one consider your site carefully and avoid putting it near trees and shrubs. Most ponds need clearing every 2–3 years.

PLANTING PLAN

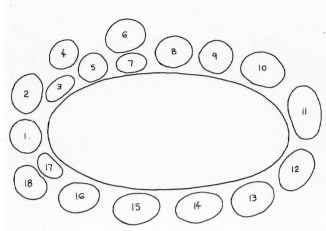

1 *Hosta* small
2 *Smilacina racemosa*
3 *Primula* sp or cv
4 *Lythrum virgatum* cv
5 *Lythrum salicaria* cv
6 *Lysimachia ephemerum*
7 *Primula* sp or cv
8 *Astilbe* sp or hybrid   s
9 *Trollius x cultorum* cv
10 *Hosta* large
11 *Dierama* sp or cv
12 *Gentiana asclepiadea*
13 *Helleborus orientalis*
14 *Liatris spicata* and cv
15 *Hosta* small
16 *Dodecatheon* sp
17 *Primula* sp or cv
18 *Ranunculus aconitifolius*
'Flore Pleno'

*HELLEBORUS ORIENTALIS is a
favourite in every garden,
producing its dog-rose-like
flowers in early to mid-spring.*

*HOSTAS both large and small,
are excellent in pondside
plantings. Their leaves are
attractive for a large part of
the year and their midsummer
flowers are simply a bonus.*

ALTERNATIVE
◦• PLANTS •◦

• A stately alternative to
Aconitum 'Newry Blue' is
A. 'Bressingham Spire',
which produces beautiful
tapering spires of deep
violet-blue flowers in
midsummer and is
furnished with glossy,
dark green leaves. If a
change of colour is
required *A.* 'Ivorine'
which has a profusion of
ivory-white flowers in
midsummer is a shorter
plant so place it nearer
the front of the border.

• Heucheras justify their
place in the border by
their foliage alone. In this
planting scheme *H.*
'Scintillation' could be
replaced successfully with
H. 'Palace Purple', a most
striking plant producing
unusual blackish-purple
leaves with an almost
metallic sheen, above
which float delicate
panicles of white flowers
in early summer.

• *Sedum spectabile*
'Brilliant', which has flat
flower heads of bright
rose-pink borne in
profusion over fleshy
grey-green leaves, could
be selected instead of *S.*
'Autumn Joy' for this
traditional scheme *S.*

• 'Ruby Glow', with its
bright rose-crimson
flowers and a height and
spread of about 12in
(30cm), would also work
well, though is perhaps
more suitable for the
front of the border.

TRADITIONAL HERBACEOUS BORDER USING ONLY EASY PERENNIALS

This is a traditional herbaceous border, planted with easy perennials and set out simply according to height and colour. None of the tall plants should require staking and there will be colour throughout the season. A few stepping stones, placed where most needed, will be helpful and are essential if the border is backed by a hedge or wall. Some of the plants, for instance the echinaceas, are best set out in groups of three as they do not 'clump up' as quickly as others, for example the *Aconitum*. You may prefer to include more than one clump of a particular plant and, if working to a tight budget, you can fill in any gaps with annuals while waiting to buy, or be given, new varieties. This plan allows for a bed of about 4.5 metres (15ft) long, but the length of the bed will depend on how closely you set out the plants. Follow the planting distances given in the Directory to allow space for the clumps to increase in size.

•· PLANTING PLAN ·•

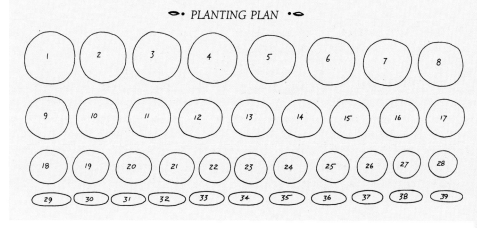

A Traditional herbaceous border – Easy perennials

1 *Aconitum* 'Newry Blue'
2 *Polemonium foliosissimum*
3 *Lythrum virgatum* 'Rose Queen'
4 *Aconitum compactum* 'Carneum'
5 *Echinacea purpurea*
6 *Echinacea purpurea* 'White Lustre'
7 *Lysimachia ephemerum*
8 *Veratrum album*
9 *Erigeron* 'Prosperity'
10 *Scabiosa* sp or hybrid
11 *Salvia* 'East Friesland'
12 *Lythrum salicaria* cv
13 *Erigeron* hybrid
14 *Cirsium japonicum*
15 *Eryngium variifolium*
16 *Filipendula vulgaris*
17 *Smilacina racemosa*
18 *Brunnera macrophylla*
19 *Gentiana asclepiadea*
20 *Incarvillea delavayi*
21 *Diascia rigescens*
22 *Liatris spicata*
23 *Sedum* 'Autumn Joy'
24 *Anaphalis triplinervis*
25 *Veronica spicata* 'Alba'
26 *Morina longifolia*
27 *Ranunculus aconitifolius* 'Flore Pleno'
28 *Euphorbia polychroma*
29 *Platycodon grandiflorus mariesii*
30 *Pulsatilla vulgaris*
31 *Primula auricula* cv
32 *Heuchera* 'Scintillation'
33 *Saxifraga x urbium*
34 *Sedum* 'Ruby Glow'
35 *Scabiosa* 'Pink Mist'
36 *Celmisia coricea*
37 *Trillium grandiflorum*
38 *Carlina acaulis caulescens*
39 *Primula auricula* cv

ALTERNATIVE ◦• *PLANTS* •◦

• Colour in the latter part of the year is particularly valued and is generously provided by the daisy-flowered asters. Instead of *Aster amellus* 'King George', as suggested in this border, try the striking *A. a.* 'Violet Queen' a very free-flowering alternative which, as its name suggests, has glorious violet flowers. A second alternative is *A. a.* 'Lady Hindlip' which produces pretty rose-pink flowers.

• For a pink alternative to the blue *Campanula lactiflore,* try *C. lactiflora* 'Loddon Anna', but place it towards the right-hand end of this border. Another clump-forming variety is *C. latifolia* which bears exquisite blue-purple flowers in high summer. This is often shorter and rarely needs staking.

• Tanacetums (Pyrethrum) are highly decorative hardy plants with large daisy-like flowers and feathery foliage and make good cut flowers, however, they do require support. *Tanacetum coccineum* has a number of cultivars so instead of the cerise-pink 'Brenda' try the bright crimson-scarlet 'Bressingham Spire' or the more subtle pale pink of 'Eileen May Robinson'.

TRADITIONAL HERBACEOUS BORDER USING BOTH EASY AND BORDERLINE PERENNIALS

A mixture of both easy and borderline plants fill this traditional border (approximately 4.5–5.5 metres (14–16ft) long). It is arranged according to height and colour, shading from blue to cream. As with the previous plan, stepping stones will make working in the border much easier and reduce the risks of standing on emerging plants in the spring, and breaking stems later in the season. Although rectangular, this bed can be adjusted for a curved border if you prefer. To achieve this, divide the third row in half and move the plants to each side of the fourth row. You may also need to move one or two plants from the first and place them at the side ot the second. (Rows are counted from front to back.)

•· PLANTING PLAN ·•

Traditional herbaceous border – Easy and borderline perennials.

* = easy
+ = borderline

1 *Campanula lactifolia* +
2 *Aconitum napellus* cv *
3 *Lychnis chalcedonica* +
4 *Sidalcea* hybrid +
5 *Lythrum virgatum* 'The Rocket' *
6 *Phlox maculata* 'Omega' +
7 *Lysimachia ephemerum* *
8 *Smilacina racemosa* *
9 *Polemonium foliosissimum* *
10 *Erigeron* hybrid *
11 *Cirsium japonicum* *
12 *Monarda didyma* +
13 *Lythrum salicaria* cv *
14 *Tanacetum coccineum* 'Brenda' +
15 *Dictamnus albus* +
16 *Solidago* hybrid *
17 *Sisyrinchium striatum* +
18 *Aster amellus* 'King George' +
19 *Gentiana asclepiadea* *
20 *Incarvillea delavayi* *
21 *Diascia rigescens* *
22 *Scabiosa rumelica* *
23 *Erigeron* hybrid *
24 *Dicentra spectabilis* +
25 *Astilbe* sp or hybrid +
26 *Achillea taygetea* +
27 *Achillea* 'Moonshine' +
28 *Geum* 'Lady Stratheden' *
29 *Nepeta* x *faasenii* +
30 *Brunnera macrophylla* *
31 *Veronica gentianoides* *
32 *Platycodon grandiflorus mariesii* *
33 *Heuchera* hybrid *
34 *Scabiosa* 'Pink Mist' *
35 *Anaphalis triplinervis* *
36 *Aconitum* 'Ivorine' *
37 *Celmisia coriacea* *
38 *Potentilla rupestris* *
39 *Trollius* hybrid *

SMALL HERBACEOUS BORDER
USING ONLY EASY PERENNIALS

This plan for a bed 2.5–3 metres (8–10ft) long, would be suitable for a small garden. Two or three stepping stones are recommended to enable easy access. The border is easily divided in half to adapt if for a long and narrow garden: the third and fourth rows could be placed against a wall and the first and second rows placed in front of climbers on another part of the wall. The plan can also be adapted to form an island bed, but in this case put the tall plants in the fourth row in the centre of the bed with rows three and two graded around them, then set the plants in row one around the edges. If you prefer a mixed bed, bulbs can be planted between the clumps; these would provide spring colour – mark their position to avoid disturbing them once the leaves have died down. (Rows are counted from front to back.)

• *Incarvillea delavayi* could be selected as a slightly taller but equally beautiful alternative to *I. mairei* in this border scheme. With its rose-red, gloxinia-like trumpets and dark green, deeply cut leaves, it provides an exotic focal point among other perennials. It seems incredible that such a tropical-looking plant can survive and thrive in cold areas with so little attention, however, a mulch is advisable in hard winters.

• The hardiness, profuse flowering and self-supporting habit of *Lythrum* make it a valuable addition to any border. Here, *L. virgatum* 'The Rocket' with deep pink flower spikes has been used, but *L. v.* 'Rose Queen' which has paler, lighter rose flowers is a worthy alternative.

• There are several species of perennial salvia, but they are not all hardy and can be short-lived plants. There are several equally attractive and easy varieties of *S. nemorosa* bearing flowers in the violet/blue range, among them *S. n.* 'East Friesland', *S. n.* 'Lubecca' and *S. n.* 'May Night'.

●• *DESIGN POINTS TO CONSIDER* •●

COLOUR   Colour is a matter of personal preference, but for really successful planting it helps to remember that to create depth and produce a natural effect it is best to use 'receding' colours (greens, blues, purples) in the background and 'advancing' colours (white, yellows, oranges, reds) in the foreground.

SHAPE   Shape in planting is just as important as colour. Unless deliberately done to achieve a particular effect, a border composed solely of round mounds is visually boring. So when planning bear in mind the overall impression of the plants: there are plants with large bold leaves, others have feathered foliage or strap-shaped leaves; variegated foliage adds interest and breaks up the all-green effect of most perennial leaves. Flowers may be born in spikes, spires or bunches.

SPECIAL INTEREST   A simple method of boosting visual impact is to include a 'specimen' plant, grown to perfection, around which less showy plants or those grown for seasonal interest, such as spring bulbs, may be positioned.

SCENT   Plants with strong perfumes beg to be displayed where the nose can best appreciate them.

THEME   When considering design think about following a theme. This may be simply one of colour or it could mimic a specific period, such as a Victorian cottage garden or Tudor knot garden.

●• *PLANTING PLAN* •●

1	2	3	4	5
6	7	8	9	10	11
12	13	14	15	16	17
18	19	20	21	22	23

Small herbaceous border – Easy perennials.

 1 *Smilacina racemosa*
 2 *Lysimachia ephemerum*
 3 *Polemonium foliosissimum*
 4 *Lythrum virgatum* 'The Rocket'
 5 *Acontium carneum* 'Compactum'
 6 *Ranunculus aconitifolius* 'Flore Pleno'
 7 *Salvia nemorosa* var
 8 *Gentian asclepiadea*
 9 *Lythrum salicaria* var
10 *Cirsium japonicum*
11 *Penstemon* hybrid
12 *Filipendula vulgaris* 'Flore Pleno'
13 *Erigeron* hybrid
14 *Scabiosa caucasica* cv
15 *Potentilla nepalensis* 'Miss Willmott'
16 *Eryngium variifolium*
17 *Erigeron* hybrid
18 *Euphorbia polychroma*
19 *Geranium renardii*
20 *Morina longifolia*
21 *Diacia rigescens*
22 *Sedum* 'Ruby Glow'
23 *Incarvillea mairei*

ALTERNATIVE
❦• PLANTS •❦

• The wonderful cottage garden look of aquilegias make them an atmospheric addition to this border. There are many hybrids available but the 'Dragonfly' and 'Music' series are particularly recommended. Their distinctive bell-shaped, long-spurred flowers, framed by ferny foliage, come in various shades of blue, yellow, red and bicolours.

• Phlox make a valuable contribution to colour in the garden in late summer, especially welcome at a time when yellows often seem to predominate. *Phlox maculata* 'Alpha' and 'Omega' both flower over a long period. 'Alpha' has broad, cylindrical heads of delicate pink flowers, while 'Omega' is white with a lilac eye. Phlox are very susceptible to ' eel-worm, so I have only included *P. maculata* – which seems to be more resistant to this pest – in the Borderline Directory.

• *Sidalcea* are graceful members of the Mallow family with waving racemes of profuse, shallow cup-shaped flowers. In this planting scheme a red or pink variety may be used and suggestions include: *S.* 'Croftway Red' – a deep pinkish-red, *S.* 'Oberon' – rose-pink, *S.* 'William Smith' – salmon-pink or *S.* 'Loveliness' – shell-pink.

SMALL HERBACEOUS BORDER USING
EASY AND BORDERLINE PERENNIALS

Another small border, 2–2.5 metres (6–8ft) long, but this time both easy and borderline perennials have been used. As with the previous plan this too can be adapted to fit into a narrow garden by dividing the rows into two beds, making stepping stones unnecessary. If you prefer you can also make the bed curved following the instructions given on page 48.

Some of the plants listed will need support – the *Lychnis chalcedonica* and the *Sidalcea* for instance. Wire herbaceous supports are ideal, but strong twigs or bamboo stakes and string can also be used. Allow ample space around the *Achillea* as this clumps up very quickly and will need dividing after two years.

❧ LAWNS ❧

<u>BEDS</u>   set into lawns can cause problems. Plants can hang over the grass making bald patches which are unsightly when dead stems or foliage are clipped back and the lawn may encroach into the bed, so a dividing line is best provided to keep the two apart. Plastic lawn edging can be bought quite cheaply but though effective, it is not aesthetically very pleasing. Stone edging looks very attractive and some of the composite bricks now available would also look well.

❧ PLANTING PLAN ❧

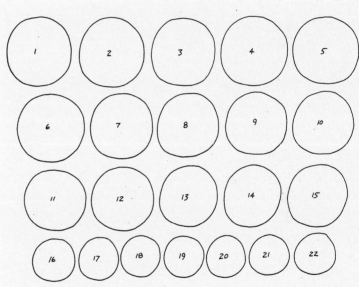

Small herbaceous border – Easy and borderline perennials.
Place stepping stones for easy access.
* = easy
+ = borderline
1 *Phlox maculata* cv +
2 *Monarda didyma* +
3 *Lychnis chalcedonica* +
4 *Sidalcea* hybrid +
5 *Campanula latifolia* +
6 *Filipendula vulgaris* *
7 *Echinacea purpurea* cv *
8 *Solidago* hybrid *
9 *Erigeron* hybrid *

10 *Aconitum* x *cammarum* var. *bicolor* *
11 *Geum* 'Lady Stratheden' *
12 *Achillea* 'Moonshine' +
13 *Doronicum austriacum* *
14 *Aquilegia* hybrid +
15 *Aster amellus* cv +
16 *Aconitum* 'Ivorine' *
17 *Coreopsis verticillata* *
18 *Trollius* x *cultorum* hybrid *
19 *Geum borisii* *
20 *Dianthus* cv or hybrid +
21 *Linum narbonense* +
22 *Nepeta* x *faasenii* +

CIRCULAR MIXED BED IN WHITE AND YELLOW
USING EASY AND BORDERLINE PERENNIALS AND BULBS

This round bed, measuring approximately 2.5–3 metres (8–10ft) across, will provide colour from spring to autumn, and the eleagnus and skimmia, being evergreen, will provide some variegated foliage for the winter months. The silvery leaves of the celmisia also remain through winter, though in severe weather they may suffer some damage. More bulbs can be planted between the clumps; small yellow tulips and daffodils and perhaps a few white hyacinths around the edges of the bed will give early colour until the shrubs and perennials start to bloom. The true *achillea taygetea* is very hard to find, but is worth searching out. Its flowers are a pale lemon yellow unlike *A.* 'Moonshine' which is bright yellow.

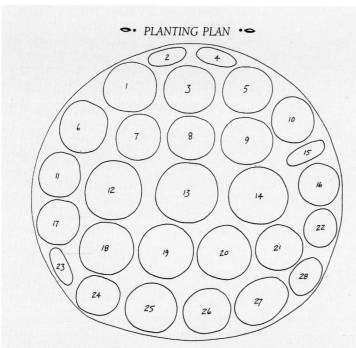

•◦ PLANTING PLAN ◦•

Circular mixed bed in white and yellow
– shrubs, easy and borderline
perennials and bulbs.

* = easy
+ = borderline

 1 *Euphorbia polychroma* *
 2 *Primula* sp *
 3 *Aconitum* 'Ivorine' *
 4 *Primula* sp *
 5 *Celmisia coriacea* *
 6 *Ballota pseudodictamnus*
 7 *Achillea taygetea* +
 8 *Coreopsis verticillata* *
 9 *Potentilla rupestris* *
10 *Helleborus niger* *
11 *Aurinia saxatilis* sp or cv *
12 *Euonymus* 'Emerald 'n Gold' (shrub)
13 *Potentilla* 'Elizabeth' (shrub)
14 *Skimmia japonica* (shrub)
15 *Narcissus* small sp or cv (bulbs)
16 *Hebe pinguifolia* 'Pagei' (shrub)
17 *Hosta* small or medium sp, hybrid
   or cv *
18 *Doronicum* sp or cv *
19 *Santolina chamaecyparissus* (shrub)
20 *Achillea* 'Moonshine' +
21 *Solidago* 'Golden Thumb' *
22 *Trollius* x *cultorum* 'Orange Princess' *
23 *Primula auricula* cv *
24 *Trollius* x *cultorum* 'Canary Bird' *
25 *Anaphalis triplinervis* *
26 *Trillium grandiflorum* *
27 *Erythronium* 'Pagoda' (bulb)

❧ PRUNING ❧

The plants in these border schemes do not require complicated or even regular pruning but some of the shrubs may need cutting back occasionally.

WHY PRUNE To keep the plant healthy and maintain a good shape; to promote upward growth and/or replacement growth; to remove old and unproductive wood; to allow air and light to reach the middle of the plant; to remove dead flowers and so save energy.

WHEN TO PRUNE If pruning _is_ necessary, allow the longest time possible for development and ripening of new growth before winter. In general, plants that flower on wood made the previous year, such as viburnums, should be pruned as soon as the flowers fade, whereas plants that flower on wood made in the current year, such as hebes, can be pruned at the end of winter.

ALTERNATIVE ❧ PLANTS ❧

• _Euonymus_ provide welcome form and colour all year. As a change from the very commonly grown _E._ 'Emerald 'n Gold' there are other forms with variegated foliage to choose from: _E._ 'Gold Tip' has green leaves edged with bright yellow, _E._ 'Sunspot' has deep green leaves, each marked centrally with golden yellow, and _E._ 'Silver Queen' which also has dark green leaves but broadly edged with white.

• The flowers of _Achillea_ are borne in erect, flat heads over pungent, deeply cut leaves in midsummer. In this circular, white and yellow scheme _A._ 'Moonshine' has been used; the smaller and paler _A. taygetea_ is a subtle and interesting option. The heads dry well if picked when fully open and before they discolour.

ALTERNATIVE
❥• PLANTS •❥

• *Dodecatheon*, with their cyclamen-like flowers, are lovely in this island bed in shades of red. All the species are well-behaved enough for the easy border. The following could be used in this scheme: *D. jeffreyi* which has red-purple flowers, *D. pulchellum* with its lavender to magenta flowers, *D. hendersonnii* which is a deep pink, or *D. meadia* which has pale pink to rose-purple flowers.

USING EASY PERENNIALS
AND SUMMER-FLOWERING BULBS

This scheme for a curved island bed of about 3–4 metres (10–12ft) long, is in shades of pink and red. The *Dierama* is placed to one side to allow its 'fishing rod' stems space to wave about in the breeze, and not interfere with neighbouring plants. There will be colour in spring with the *Lychnis flos-jovis*, auricula primulas and dodecatheon, and other plants will continue to provide colour right through the summer, ending with the lythrum and last of all, the nerines in autumn. Remember to mark the position of the bulbs, or make a note of their position in your garden record book to avoid accidentally digging them up when clearing up the bed in autumn or spring.

As with the previous plan, an edging to the bed is recommended: there is always a problem with clipping grass edges, each time you clip or cut around them you soften the line of the bed and you will find the width of the border will gradually increase over the years until the original outline has been lost. Clippers or a strimmer can be used along the edging to keep the grass neat.

•ᴗ PLANTING PLAN ᴗ•

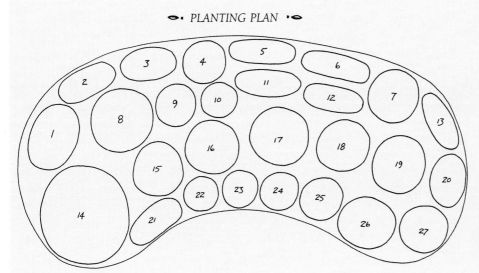

F Island bed – Easy perennials and bulbs.

1 *Penstemon* hybrid
2 *Heuchera sanguinea*
3 *Incarvillea delavayi*
4 *Potentilla nepalensis* 'Miss Willmott'
5 *Saxifraga x urbium*
6 *Armeria pseudoarmeria* 'Bees Hybrid'
7 *Veronica spicata* 'Red Fox'
8 *Erigeron* hybrid
9 *Nerine bowdenii* (bulb)
10 *Allium aflatunense* (bulb)
11 *Scabiosa rumelica*
12 *Gladiolus byzantinus* (corm)
13 *Heuchera* hybrid
14 *Dierama pulcherrimum*
15 *Aconitum compactum* 'Carneum'
16 *Lythrum salicaria* 'The Rocket'
17 *Penstemon* hybrid
18 *Cirsium japonicum*
19 *Liatris spicata*
20 *Dodecatheon sp*
21 *Diascia rigescens*
22 *Lychnis flos-jovis*
23 *Primula auricula* hybrid
24 *Trillium erectum*
25 *Helleborus orientalis*
26 *Sedum* 'Ruby Glow'
27 *Morina longifolia*

ALTERNATIVE
•ᴗ PLANTS ᴗ•

• The *Primula* genus is huge and so is its colour range, but this island scheme calls for one in a red shade. A visit to your local garden centre should yield plenty of choice, for example: *P. auricula* 'Red Dusty Miller' or *P. a.* 'The Mikado'.

ALTERNATIVE
❧ PLANTS ☙

• *Cyclamen* are truly
delightful plants, bringing
welcome colour in
midwinter or late
summer and autumn.
Most species produce
flowers in a range of reds
and pinks but white
forms are available. The
variety *C. hederifolium
album* has pure white
flowers appearing before
or with the leaves, which
are patterned in
silvery-grey and often ivy
leaf-shaped.

ALL WHITE ISLAND BED USING
SHRUBS, BULBS AND EASY PERENNIALS

An all white colour scheme is very attractive in a garden, providing a cool antidote to the hot strident colours of high summer. In this plan, spring interest comes from the graceful, long-lasting leucojums, which resemble giant snowdrops, and the primroses, trilliums, pulsatillas and the *Primula denticulata*. More bulbs – white hyacinths, small tulips and daffodils – and more primroses can be fitted in gaps around the edges of the bed. There are some lovely double varieties of primrose available, and these would do well in any more shaded part of the bed. This plan is for a bed 3–4 metres (10–12ft) long; if yours is the same size you may wish to place some stepping stones once the plants are established. A thick mulch of a layer of fine bark or coconut chippings will help to keep the bed weed free and conserve moisture. Apply this after rain, or water the bed well beforehand.

❧ PLANTING PLAN ❧

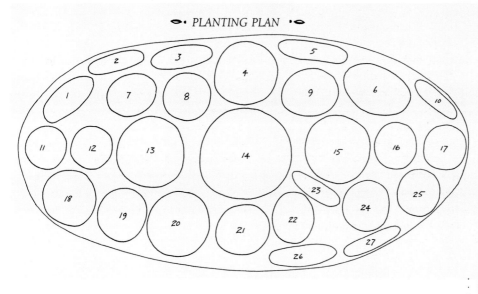

All white island bed –
shrubs, easy perennials and
bulbs.
1 *Heuchera* 'Pearl Drops'
2 *Primula* cv
3 *Helleborus niger*
4 *Smilacina racemosa*
5 *Cyclamen* sp
6 *Morina longifolia*
7 *Ranunculus aconitifolius*
   'Flore Pleno'
8 *Galtonia candicans*
9 *Veronica spicata* 'Alba'
10 *Primula* cv
11 *Celmisia coriacea*
12 *Anaphalis triplinervis*
13 *Philadelphus microphyllus*
14 *Viburnum carlesii*
15 *Potentilla fruticosa* 'Tilford
   Cream' (shrub)
16 *Liatris spicata* 'Album'
17 *Trillium grandiflorum*
18 *Pulsatilla alpina* subsp.
   apiifolium
19 *Scabiosa caucasica* 'Miss
   Willmott'
20 *Hosta* small or medium
21 *Iris* (bulb)
22 *Potentilla rupestris*
23 *Leucojum aestivum* (bulb)
24 *Aconitum* 'Ivorine'
25 *Hosta* small
26 *Heuchera* 'Palace Purple'
27 *Primula denticulata*

• Shrubby potentillas are
colourful and easy plants,
now available in a wide
range of colours. An
excellent alternative to
the creamy-white *P.
fruticosa* 'Tilford Cream' is
P. 'Abbotswood', an
impressive plant with
large, pure white flowers.

• Charming members of
the herbaceous or mixed
border, *Scabious* are also
wonderful for floral
decorations. White forms
are an interesting change
to the more common
blue shades. For an
alternative to *S. caucasica*
'Miss Willmott', try the
lovely *S. c.* 'Bressingham
White'.

MIXED BED USING
SHRUBS, BULBS, EASY BORDERLINE PERENNIALS

This mixed bed of easy shrubs, bulbs and perennials is laid out to be backed by a wall or hedge and measures 2.5–3 metres (8–10ft) long. Remember to leave room at the back of it, especially if it is behind a hedge. You will need to be able to get at the hedge to clip it; do not plant the shrubs too close to it, as hedges take a lot of moisture from the soil. This bed is best positioned facing the sun, the wall giving shelter from cold winds and allowing maximum sunshine to reach the plants. Stepping stones will be necessary: place them once the plants are established and it is easier to see where they are most needed. The viburnum can be pruned when necessary to keep it a manageable size; the skimmia and gaultheria will probably only require the removal of a few untidy pieces in the spring, and light clipping over the potentilla will keep this neat.

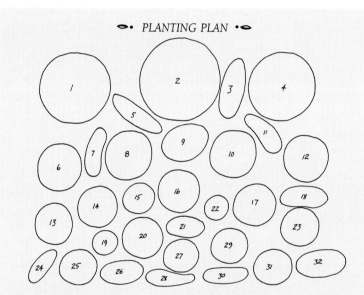

•• PLANTING PLAN ••

Mixed border shrubs, easy and borderline perennials, and bulbs.

* = easy
\+ = borderline

1 *Gaultheria mucronata* (shrub)
2 *Viburnum carlesii* (shrub)
3 *Allium giganticum* (bulb)
4 *Skimmia japonica* (shrub)
5 *Camassia* sp (bulb)
6 *Euonymus fortunei* cv (shrub)
7 *Camassia* sp (bulb)
8 *Paeonia* sp +
9 *Galtonia candicans* (bulb)
10 *Potentilla* sp (shrub)
11 *Allium aflatunense* (bulb)
12 *Hebe armstrongii* 'Autumn Glory' (shrub)
13 *Agapanthus* 'Headbourne Hybrids' +
14 *Ballota pseudodictamnus* (shrub)
15 *Nerine bowdenii* (bulb)
16 *Daphne tangutica* Retusa group (shrub)
17 *Euphorbia polychroma* *
18 *Leucojum aestivum* (bulb)
19 *Iris* hybrid (bulb)
20 *Helleborus orientalis* hybrid *
21 *Fritillaria meleagris* (bulb)
22 *Iris* hybrid (bulb)
23 *Hebe pinguifolia* 'Pagei' (shrub)
24 *Tulipa* small sp or hybrids (bulb)
25 *Primula auricula* hybrid *
26 *Cyclamen* sp *
27 *Anaphalis triplinervis* *
28 *Erythronium* sp or hybrid (bulb)
29 *Linum narbonense* +
30 *Brodiaea coronaria* (bulb)
31 *Ruta graveolens* 'Jackman's Blue' (shrub)
32 *Narcissus* small sp and hybrids (bulb)

⚬· PLANTING BULBS ·⚬

Plant bulbs between herbaceous perennials, the emerging foliage of these will help to hide any persistent bulb leaves after flowering and fill gaps left when the bulbs have finished flowering. Most bulbs should be planted when they are dormant: early autumn for spring-flowering bulbs, early spring for summer-flowering ones. As a general rule they should be planted in a hole of twice their own depth (for a bulb 5cm (2in) high make a hole 10cm (4in) deep), deeper if the soil is light, sandy or very dry. Nearly all bulbs resent damp conditions, and will rot in heavy, wet soils. Make sure, *before* you plant them, that the soil and site is suitable for the bulb: some like free draining soil and sunshine, others prefer some light shade and a more retentive soil. If your soil is very heavy, work in plenty of coarse sand and fine gravel, and put a handful of sharp sand in the bottom of the hole on which the bulb can be placed to prevent it rotting. Ensure the soil is fertile by adding a low nitrogen, high potash and phosphate fertiliser, such as bonemeal, before planting.

ALTERNATIVE ⚬· PLANTS ·⚬

• For real impact in a border try one of the *Paeonia lactiflora* varieties. These are the largest-flowered peonies and are mostly doubles, of which pink P. 'Sarah Bernhardt' is a good example. Others to try include, P. 'Duchesse de Nemours', creamy-white and deliciously scented, P. 'Karl Rosenfeld', bold crimson and P. 'Bowl of Beauty', pink with a clustered centre of creamy-white. Remember that these will require support.

• The choice of Tulips is bewildering and with so many to choose from it may be easier to pot up a selection in the autumn and place them in the border when they flower – either for short-term impact, or for permanent planting if the colour and shape suits. *Tulipa kaufmanniana* is available in many colours, its oval petals opening wide to the sun. Alternatively try the species *T. batalinii*, a short, early-flowering tulip in the yellow-orange-red range. There are also several lovely hybrids between *T. batalinii* and *T. linifolia*, including 'Apricot Jewel', orange-red outside and yellow inside, and 'Bright Gem', which has yellow flowers with an orange flush.

ALTERNATIVE •· PLANTS ·•

• The *Fritillaria* genus has many members but for the purposes of this mixed bed the shorter varieties are suggested. *F. meleagris* is popular, with its unusual chequered flowers in white or reddish-purple, but *F. pallidiflora* is actually one of the best species for the open garden and has broad glaucous leaves with greenish-cream to yellow flowers. *F. pontica* may also be used, having greenish-yellow flowers marked with purplish-brown.

• A shrubby veronica, *Hebe armstrongii* 'Autumn Glory' has been used in this scheme but other hebes may be used instead. *H. albicans* has white flowers which would perfectly complement the smaller-growing *Hebe pinguifolia* 'Pagei' in front or, in milder areas, try less hardy hebes, such as *H. macrantha*, or one of the many colourful hybrids like *H.* 'E. A. Bowles'.

• The lush, distinctive foliage of *Hosta* is irresistible, making a bold statement in the border. Any of the small to medium varieties would create an impact in this scheme. The foliage of *H. undulata* is stunning, being a fresh mid-green splashed with white or cream markings. *H.* 'Blue Moon' is coolly impressive with its blue-green leaves and mauve flowers, while *H. lancifolia* has lush dark green leaves above which rise purple flowers.

CORNER BED USING SHRUBS, BULBS AND HOSTAS

This corner bed, ideally in a walled garden, has a planting of shrubs and bulbs, with a few hostas in the shaded corner. It has been designed for a minimum amount of work, so a thick mulch of fine bark or coconut chippings is essential to suppress weeds and conserve moisture. The short sides measure about 3–4 metres (10–12ft) so stepping stones will be needed. More bulbs can be added as required, and some perennial plants introduced if you wish to have these in the bed. Rue can cause a painful rash on unprotected skin in some people, so do wear disposable gloves when planting, or handling the foliage, and if you have children do not plant it in your garden. There is a charming new small hebe called 'Rosie' which would make a good substitute, or *H. pinguifolia* 'Pagei' which has grey leaves, would also be suitable.

•· PLANTING PLAN ·•

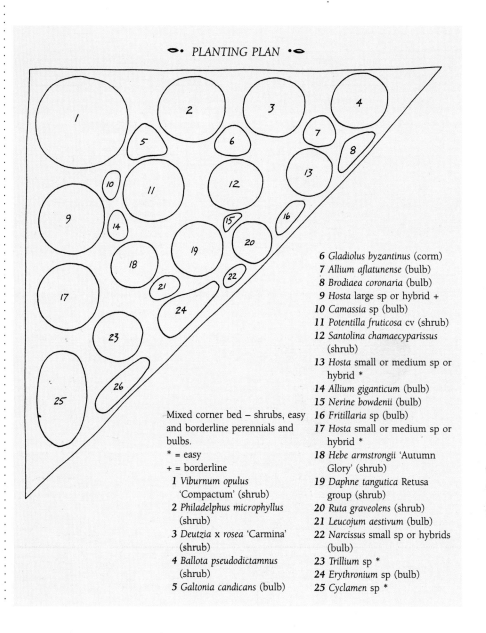

Mixed corner bed – shrubs, easy and borderline perennials and bulbs.

* = easy
\+ = borderline

1 *Viburnum opulus* 'Compactum' (shrub)
2 *Philadelphus microphyllus* (shrub)
3 *Deutzia x rosea* 'Carmina' (shrub)
4 *Ballota pseudodictamnus* (shrub)
5 *Galtonia candicans* (bulb)
6 *Gladiolus byzantinus* (corm)
7 *Allium aflatunense* (bulb)
8 *Brodiaea coronaria* (bulb)
9 *Hosta* large sp or hybrid +
10 *Camassia* sp (bulb)
11 *Potentilla fruticosa* cv (shrub)
12 *Santolina chamaecyparissus* (shrub)
13 *Hosta* small or medium sp or hybrid *
14 *Allium giganticum* (bulb)
15 *Nerine bowdenii* (bulb)
16 *Fritillaria* sp (bulb)
17 *Hosta* small or medium sp or hybrid *
18 *Hebe armstrongii* 'Autumn Glory' (shrub)
19 *Daphne tangutica* Retusa group (shrub)
20 *Ruta graveolens* (shrub)
21 *Leucojum aestivum* (bulb)
22 *Narcissus* small sp or hybrids (bulb)
23 *Trillium* sp *
24 *Erythronium* sp (bulb)
25 *Cyclamen* sp *

❧· BULB CARE ·❧

AFTER FLOWERING Never cut off the leaves of bulbs before these have died down. It is tempting to do this when they turn brown at the ends and look unsightly, but the bulbs need to take in sunlight and water to build up strength for the next season. Do not tie the leaves up as this has the same ill effect.

NOTE Remember to make a note of where you have planted the bulbs; I often forget to do this and, finding a gap in the border later in the season, dig a hole in which to place a container-grown plant, only to find I am digging up large clumps of bulbs!

STORAGE If bulbs are to be lifted and stored, do this after the foliage has died down. Clean them up, dip them in fungicide to discourage disease, place them in shallow trays and cover them with peat. Label clearly and store in a cool, frost-free place. Check them regularly, removing any that rot or show disease.

Plant Directories

There are four directories: Easy Perennials – a selection of the best trouble-free, non-invasive perennials; Borderline Perennials – plants on the whole easy to grow, but with one or two bad habits; finally, the Shrub Directory and the Bulb Directory – plants suitable for mixed borders. All have been grown in my garden, with the exception of one or two recommended by friends who vouch for their good behaviour.

DIRECTORY OF EASY PERENNIALS

≈❧ *ACONITUM* ❧≈

Ranunculaceae
HELMET FLOWER
MONK'S HOOD
WOLF'S BANE

The name *Aconitum* comes from the Anglo-Saxon 'aconita thung', meaning deadly poison – all parts of the plant are poisonous. The pollen of *Aconitum lycoctonum* was used on the tips of arrows and to poison bait for wolves, hence the name Wolf's Bane. The flowers resemble a monk's cowl – another of its common names. Dr. Stoerck, a German physician, discovered the medicinal properties of this plant, which led to it being used in the treatment of rheumatism and heart conditions.

It is useful to us, however, for a different reason; it is one of the very few tall plants that do not need staking, and is invaluable for the back of the easy border.

There are quite a few species of *Aconitum*, one of the best known is *A. napellus*, which has been a cottage-garden plant for many centuries. It grows to 1.5m (5ft), with a spread of 30cm (12in), and has indigo-blue flowers. The following are all easily obtained from good nurseries. They are all neat-growing and non-invasive, forming clumps that gradually increase in size. When they get too big they are very easy to lift and divide.

A. 'Newry Blue' has dark blue flowers: *A.* 'Bressingham Spire' has violet-blue flowers and *A.* x *cammarum* var. *bicolor* has flowers of purple and white. *A. compactum* 'Carneum' has salmon-pink flowers, and does well in colder gardens. These grow to 1-1.2m (3-4ft) high, spread to 50cm (20in), and flower in midsummer.

A. 'Ivorine' has small cream flowers in early summer. It grows to 30-45cm (12-18in) with a spread of 50cm (20in). There are other species available, some of which have yellow flowers. These may be suitable for the easy border but I am unable to vouch for their habits.

• CULTIVATION *Aconitum* likes good rich soil, which will not dry out, and a mulch of compost or well-rotted manure in the spring. Plant in partial shade, or in full sun if they are to go into well-mulched, retentive soil. They start into growth early and can be planted out anytime between autumn and spring. Allow 30-45cm (12-18in)

ACONITUM NAPELLUS

between *A.* 'Ivorine' and 45-60cm (18-24in) between the others listed here. Feed with blood, fish and bone, or general-purpose fertiliser, if required. Deadhead the flower stems, and cut down the spent foliage in the autumn. They can be grown from seed. Sow in early spring in a cold frame or cold greenhouse. (See Propagation p.28.)

• *PESTS AND DISEASES* Usually trouble free.

• *BONUS POINTS* *Aconitum* dries well if cut when all but the top two or three flowers have opened. Hang upside down in bunches over a boiler or in an airing cupboard for a few days.

. . . .

ANAPHALIS

Compositae

PEARLY EVERLASTING

There are several forms of *Anaphalis*, but the best for the well-behaved border is *A. triplinervis*, which forms a neat clump of grey-green leaves and produces tight heads of small white flowers in mid- to late summer. It is useful in the front of the border, reaching 30-38cm (12-15in). The clumps increase gradually to about 60cm (24in) across and are reasonably easy to lift and divide.

• *CULTIVATION* Plant in either spring or autumn in well-drained soil. Provide some humus as it does not like its roots to dry out. A sunny position is best, but partial shade will be tolerated. Feeding is not usually necessary. If the clumps get too large, lift them and use the young, outer parts for replanting. *Anaphalis* can be grown from seed. Sow in early spring in a tray and put in a cold frame.

• *PESTS AND DISEASES* Usually trouble free.

ANAPHALIS TRIPLINERVIS

• *BONUS POINTS* Flowers dry well if picked before the heads open too far and become fluffy. Hang upside down to dry and, once dry, keep them out of damp rooms.

. . . .

ARMERIA

Plumbaginaceae

THRIFT

The name thrift derives from the verb 'threave', meaning to keep together, and the plants, with their short, thin leaves live up to their name by forming very neat clumps.

Armeria arenaria is highly recommended for the easy border. I grew mine from seed many years ago and

many are still in the same clumps in the border, although some have been lifted and divided. Those still in their original positions have never given me a moments trouble. Although this species is not commercially available at present the similar *Armeria pseudoarmeria* 'Bees Hybrids' is a good alternative. It produces ball-shaped heads of red or pink flowers in early summer. The flowers are on strong stems 60cm (24in) tall, and are very long lasting. If the stems are cut off when the flowers have faded, the plant will often produce a second flush later on. There is now a white form available, which is also most attractive.

• *CULTIVATION* Plant either in spring or autumn, in well-drained soil and full sun. Allow 30-45cm (12-18in) between plants. Feeding is usually unnecessary.

• *PESTS AND DISEASES* Usually trouble free.

• *BONUS POINTS* It is very easy to grow from seed. In early spring, sow seeds in a tray and place in a cold frame or a cool greenhouse. Prick out into pots using a loam-based compost and plant out in late summer.

· · · · · · · · · · · · · · · · ·

❧! *AURINIA* 🌿

Cruciferae

GOLD DUST

Aurinia is usually classified as a rock plant, but it is excellent for the front of the border. *Aurinia saxatilis* (syn. *Alyssum saxatile*) flowers in spring. Its heads of golden flowers are charming and if they are cut away when they are over, the plant will produce a second, and sometimes a third flush later on in the season. The flower stems grow from 22-60cm (9-12in) in height and the plant may reach 45-60cm (18-24in) across. The leaves are evergreen, but can get rather bedraggled in the winter. However, the clumps soon recover in the spring. Var. *citrina* has pale yellow flowers; 'Flore Pleno' has double, golden yellow heads; and 'Variegata' has grey-green leaves with cream edges.

• *CULTIVATION* Plant between autumn and spring in ordinary, well-drained soil in a sunny position. Remove all dead flowerheads regularly, and trim away any long, lanky leaf stems to keep the clump neat. *Aurinia* is very easy to grow from seed. In spring sow in a tray in a warm greenhouse. Prick out the seedlings

when large enough to handle and plant in 8cm (3in) pots, harden off and plant out when all danger of frost has passed.

• *PESTS AND DISEASES* Usually trouble free.

• *BONUS POINTS* *Aurinia*, with its repeat flowering, is a 'good value' plant.

· · · · · · · · · · · · · · · · ·

❧! *BRUNNERA* 🌿

Boraginaceae

SIBERIAN BUGLOSS

Some books recommend *Brunnera macrophylla* as groundcover, but mine have never shown any inclination to wander, perhaps because they are in a rather dry part of the border.

B. macrophylla is a delight in the spring with its bright blue 'forget-me-not' flowers and when the dead flower stems have been removed the leaves are still attractive. The plant

grows to 30-45cm (12-18in) and spreads to 60cm (24in).

• *CULTIVATION* Plant either in autumn or spring, in ordinary soil, in sun or partial shade. Add some compost or moisture-retaining humus if your soil is light and apt to dry out in summer. The clumps can be lifted and divided, or root cuttings may be taken in the autumn and grown on in a cold frame until the following spring.

• *PESTS AND DISEASES* Usually trouble free.

• *BONUS POINTS* 'Forget-me-not' flowers without the trouble of raising annual plants.

· · · · · · · · · · · · · · · · ·

❧! *CARLINA* 🌿

Compositae

CARLINE THISTLE

Carlina acaulis caulescens is a most striking and unusual plant. It

BRUNNERA MACROPHYLLA

forms a neat clump of prickly leaves, 30-45cm (12-18in) in width, from which it produces, in mid- to late summer, stems 20-45cm (8-18in) tall, bearing beige, thistle-like heads. These are very attractive to bees, which become drowsy and sometimes die after feeding off the flowers. I have been unable to find what it is that causes this reaction. The flowers are very long lasting, and they dry beautifully.

• *CULTIVATION* *Carlina* likes ordinary, very well-drained soil, and a sunny position. If your soil is heavy, work in plenty of grit before setting out the plants, which is best done in the spring. They are almost impossible to divide, having long tap roots, but are relatively easy to grow, if you can find a source of good, fresh seed. If you want the heads for cutting be sure to get the variety *caulescens* as this produces stems of a good length.

• *PESTS AND DISEASES* Trouble free, but they do not enjoy very wet winters.

• *BONUS POINTS* It dries well. Pick (use gloves!) when the petals are beginning to open, cut away some of the lower leaves, keeping a few to form a 'ruff' around the flower, and bunch in groups of 3-5 stems and hang up to dry in warm room.

❧ CELMISIA ❧
Compositae

Celmisia coriacea forms neat semi-evergreen clumps of grey-green leaves, which are woolly on the undersides. White, daisy-like flowers are produced on single stems; 30-40cm (12-16in) high, in early summer. It is a very easy plant, and apart from pulling off any dead leaves, requires no attention at all. If the clumps get too large, lift and

divide them, replanting the young, outer portions and discarding the older, central sections.

• *CULTIVATION* *Celmisia* likes well-drained soil, which contains some humus. Plant in autumn or spring. Allow 30-45cm (12-18in) between plants. Feeding is not usually necessary.

• *PESTS AND DISEASES* Trouble free.

• *BONUS POINTS* One of the few herbaceous plants that does not die down in the winter.

CIRSIUM JAPONICUM

❧ CIRSIUM ❧
Compositae

Cirsium japonicum is an unusual plant belonging to the thistle family. It produces 45-60cm (18-24in) stems with prickly leaves and, in mid- to late summer, small, dark red or pink thistle-like flowerheads.

• *CULTIVATION* It is easily grown from seed and usually flowers in its first season. Sow in spring in a greenhouse or cold frame, thinning out into sectioned trays or small pots. Harden off and plant out either singly or in groups of three,

25-30cm (10-12in) apart, when all danger of frost has passed, in well-drained soil and a sunny position.

• *PESTS AND DISEASES* Usually trouble free.

• *BONUS POINTS* The flowers dry well. Pick when fully formed and hang upside down in bunches in a warm room.

❧ COREOPSIS ❧
Compositae

Most *Coreopsis* are short-lived plants, and have to be propagated regularly by seed. *C. verticillata*, which reaches 45-60cm (18-24in) in height with a spread of 30cm (12in), is reputed to be long lasting, but cannot be relied upon to be truly perennial. It is, however, very easy to raise from seed. It is included in this directory because of its decorative value. Just one plant, purchased at the beginning of the season, will reward you with bright yellow daisies all summer and it may well survive the winter.

• *CULTIVATION* Plant is spring in any ordinary garden soil in a sunny position. Seed can be sown in a tray in spring and placed in a cold frame. Prick out the seedlings, when large enough to handle, into small pots, and transfer the plants to their permanent positions when they are growing strongly.

• *PESTS AND DISEASES* Usually trouble free.

❧ DIASCIA ❧
Scrophulariaceae

Diascia rigescens is a delightful plant, which has only become popular and easy to obtain in the last few years. It is my favourite perennial, and seemingly also everyone

COREOPSIS VERTICILLATA

• *CULTIVATION* *Diascia* likes a sunny position and good rich soil which drains well. Although they are not entirely hardy in very cold areas or in severe winters, they are very easy to propagate. In late summer take some new, unflowering shoots, about 15-20cm (6-8in) long, and put groups of four or five into polystyrene cups filled with a mixture of perlite and water. Make sure the perlite is always kept wet. In 4-6 weeks the cuttings will have rooted and can be potted on. They are best kept in the greenhouse over the winter, then hardened off in spring and planted out when all danger of frost has passed. Most winters the plants will survive outside, but it is sensible to be sure of having replacements if needed – any surplus ones will always be in demand.

• *PESTS AND DISEASES* Usually trouble free.

• *BONUS POINTS* A versatile, delightful plant with no vices, which is useful in both the border and containers.

. . . .

❧ *DIERAMA* ☙

Iridaceae

WAND FLOWER

ANGEL'S FISHING ROD

*D*ierama pulcherrimum has evergreen, sword-shaped leaves, similar to those of an iris. In late summer it produces long arching stems, resembling fishing rods, which carry a series of bright pink, trumpet-shaped flowers. A most unusual plant, it is charming to watch as the stems sway and bob in the breeze. It can grow to 1-1.5m (3-5ft) in height, with a spread of 30-40cm (12-16in), but does not need staking. It is now available in

else's. Visitors invariably exclaim, 'What is that plant?' swiftly followed by, 'Please may I have a cutting?', on seeing it for the first time.

D. rigescens has semi-evergreen leaves, and graceful sprays of small, tubular, pink flowers. These are very long lasting and, if cut back to half when the flowers have faded, will produce another flush. The plant forms a neat clump 30-50cm (12-20in) high and 30-40cm (12-16in) across. Although the

sprays do tend to fall over, this is no problem as they are so light they do no damage to neighbouring plants and they look most attractive mingling with other flowers. *Diascia* also makes a first-rate pot plant.

There are other varieties including *D. vigilis* (syn. *D. elegans*) which in my opinion does not entirely live up to its name. It has paler pink flowers and, being inclined to wander, does not form such a neat clump as *D. rigescens*.

DIERAMA PULCHERRIMUM

other colours, such as white, purple and red.

D. pendulum is similar, though taller – indeed there seems to be some confusion over which of these species is the Angel's or Venus' Fishing Rod.

• *CULTIVATION* Dieramas are hardy in all but the coldest of areas or winters and can be obtained from good nurseries. They like good rich soil which contains plenty of humus and remains moist in summer. If you have a pool, plant a *Dierama* beside it so that the 'fishing rods' can hang over the water.

It is best to plant them in the spring. They are very easy to grow from seed and, as they resent disturbance, this is the best way to increase them. If necessary, they can also be propagated by lifting the plants and carefully breaking off the little offshoots, but these will take several years to get established.

• *PESTS AND DISEASES* Trouble free.

• *BONUS POINTS* Produce seed that is easy to grow.

❧ DODECATHEON ❧
Primulaceae
SHOOTING STAR

There are several species of *Dode-catheon*, all of which are recommended. Their pink or red flowers are similar to those of the cyclamen. They flower in spring or early summer and make small, neat-growing clumps, 12-45cm (6-18in) across, with stems 20-45cm (8-18in) tall, according to species.

• *CULTIVATION* Plant 30cm (12in) apart in good, rich soil that contains plenty of humus, but is well-drained. Mulch with well-rotted manure or leaf mould in late winter. *Dodecatheon* can be grown from seed sown in late summer or spring. Place the tray in a cold frame, and prick out seedlings into small pots when large enough to handle. They will not be ready for planting out for two years.

• *PESTS AND DISEASES* Trouble free.

❧ DORONICUM ❧
Compositae
LEOPARD'S BANE

The genus *Doronicum* has several species, all producing yellow

DIASCIA RIGESCENS

DORONICUM CORDATUM

daisies in early spring and summer.

The dried roots of D. *plantagineum* were used in earlier times to poison predatory animals and vermin, hence its name Leopard's Bane. The botanist Conrad Gesner is reputed to have killed himself by taking an experimental dose.

Doronicum x *excelsum* has two good varieties – 'Harpur Crewe' and 'Miss Mason'. They both form clumps 30-45cm (12-18in) across and 60cm (24in) in height.

D. *austriacum*, which grows to 45-60cm (18-24in) in height and has a spread of 60cm (24in), is probably the most commonly grown. Its bright yellow flowers are a delight, being among the first to appear in spring. Care is needed after flowering, because the plant tends to die down and it is easy to disturb the roots when weeding.

D. *cordatum*, syn. D. *columnae*, is a smaller, neater species 30cm (12in) high with a similar spread.

• *CULTIVATION* Plant between autumn and spring in good, moisture-retentive soil, in sun or partial shade. Divide and replant as necessary.

• *PESTS AND DISEASES* The leaves can be affected by powdery mildew, but otherwise they are trouble free.

• *BONUS POINTS* One of the first flowers to bloom in the spring and excellent for early arrangements.

. . . .

❧ *ECHINACEA* ❧

Compositae

CONE FLOWER

*E*chinacea purpurea used to be called *Rudbeckia purpurea* and may still be found in nurseries under this name. It is a very handsome plant, producing tall stems 60cm-1.2m (2-4ft) in height in clumps 45cm (18in) wide. The dark pink, daisy-like flowers are borne in late summer. The crimson-pink 'Robert Bloom' is also recommended, and 'White Lustre', which has white flowers.

The flowers of all these are long lasting and they do not need staking.

• *CULTIVATION* Plant in full sun and good, rich, well-drained soil, in spring or autumn. Allow 30-45cm (12-18in) between the plants. Mulch in spring with well-rotted manure or compost. Feed with blood, fish and bone or general-purpose fertiliser. In warm areas where plants may grow well they can be lifted and divided as necessary. It can be grown from seed.

• *PESTS AND DISEASES* Trouble free.

• *BONUS POINTS* Echinacea provide welcome colour for the border in late summer.

. . . .

❧ *ERIGERON* ❧

Compositae

FLEABANE

*T*here are several species of *Erigeron*, but the most popular plants are the cultivars and hybrids that used to be listed under E. *speciosus*. These include E. 'Dignity' with lilac flowers, E. 'Dunkelste Aller' (syn 'Darkest of All'), which has violet flowers, E. 'Felicity' with light pink flowers, the semi-double, blue-flowered E. 'Prosperity', and the light mauve-pink E. 'Quakeress'.

These all make neat clumps, 45-60cm (18-24in) high and 30-45cm (12-18in) across. They freely produce daisy-like flowers in midsummer and are long lasting and trouble free. Although they sometimes flop, a few twigs or a wire

ERIGERON 'QUAKERESS'

frame will provide enough support –
well worth the effort.

• *CULTIVATION* *Erigeron* likes good,
rich soil that is well-drained, and a
sunny position. Like most
herbaceous perennials, it enjoys a
mulch of compost each spring; if
feeding is necessary, either blood,
fish and bone, or a general-purpose
fertiliser can be applied at the same
time. When the flowers fade, cut
off the dead heads, and a second
flush may well appear in late
summer. Plant either in spring or
autumn. The clumps should be
divided every three or four years.
This is very easily done; use the
young, outer portions for
replanting. Allow 30-60cm
(12-24in) between plants. Can be
raised from seed if required.
• *PESTS AND DISEASES* Trouble free.
• *BONUS POINTS* Long lasting as cut
flowers, and provide a whole range
of colours and are invaluable in the
border.

ERYNGIUM VARIIFOLIUM

❧ *ERYNGIUM* ❧
Umbelliferae

There are more than sixteen species of hardy eryngiums, but the
only one recommended for the easy
border is *E. variifolium*, which makes
a neat, slow-growing clump with
grey-green leaves that are marbled
with white veins, and is evergreen in
mild areas. It produces stems 45cm
(18in) tall bearing grey, spiky heads
in midsummer. It spreads to
45-60cm (18-24in) across.

• *CULTIVATION* Plant either in spring
or summer in any reasonable soil
that is well-drained and in a sunny
position. Feeding is not usually
necessary.
• *PESTS AND DISEASES* Trouble free.
• *BONUS POINTS* A long-lasting
flower which can be dried, but not
as successfully as other varieties.

❧ *EUPHORBIA* ❧
Euphorbiaceae
SPURGE

There are many species of
Euphorbia, most of which are
very attractive but, with the exception of the one listed, all are invasive,
and therefore not suitable for the
easy border; some are also very tall.

E. polychroma is very well
behaved, forming a neat clump
45cm (18in) high and 45-60cm
(18-24in) across, and producing yel-
low-green bracts in heads 8cm (3in)
across in early spring. In mild areas it
is evergreen.

All *Euphorbia* produce a white,
milky sap when cut. This can irritate
sensitive skins so wear gloves when
cutting the stems; if using the flowers
for arranging, burn the ends of the
stems to seal the sap in.

• *CULTIVATION* Plant between

GENTIANA ASCLEPIADEA

autumn and spring in ordinary, well-drained soil, in a sunny position. The clumps can be divided in the autumn, and young portions replanted.

• *PESTS AND DISEASES* Usually trouble free.

• *BONUS POINTS* *E. polychroma* flowers in the spring making a charming accompaniment for daffodils in flower arrangements.

. . . .

❧ *FILIPENDULA* ❧

Rosaceae

There are several species of *Fili-pendula*, but *F. vulgaris* (syn. *F. hexapetala*), known as Dropwort, is the best for the easy border, especially the variety 'Flore Plena'. This makes a neat clump, 45cm (18in) across, of fern-like leaves, which in midsummer produces charming heads of double, creamy-white flowers on 45-60cm (18-24in)

stems. It does not need staking, although heavy rain or gales can topple the flowers.

———————————

• *CULTIVATION* *F. vulgaris* likes a sunny position and ordinary, preferably alkaline, soil. Allow 45cm (18in) between plants. It can be grown from seed.

• *PESTS AND DISEASES* Usually trouble free, although the leaves can be affected by powdery mildew.

• *BONUS POINTS* Resembling wild Meadowsweet, to which family it belongs, *Filipendula* has a delicious scent.

. . . .

❧ *GENTIANA* ❧

Gentianaeae

GENTIAN

Gentiana asclepiadea (Willow Gentian) is one of my most favourite plants, in mid- to late summer producing glorious dark

blue, trumpet-shaped flowers. It may need some support if placed in an exposed position, but it is well worth this extra attention. Pale blue and white varieties are now available. The plants reach 45-60cm (18-24in) in height with a spread of 60cm (24in).

———————————

• *CULTIVATION* Willow Gentian prefers some shade and a damp, moisture-retentive soil, but will grow in almost any position. Mine, which seems perfectly happy, is placed in a sunny position at the edge of my bog garden. Clumps can be divided in early spring, and it can be raised from seed.

• *PESTS AND DISEASES* Usually trouble free.

• *BONUS POINTS* A delightful plant that provides welcome blue colour in the border in mid- to late summer.

. . . .

GERANIUM

Geraniaceae

CRANESBILL

There are a great many species of *Geranium* (not to be confused with the summer bedding plants, *Pelargonium*) but not all are well behaved. The name Cranesbill refers to the long seed pods; at one time the leaves were thought to reduce the flow of blood from wounds. Recommended for the easy border is *G. renardii* which makes a neat clump 30cm (12in) in height and spread, of attractive sage-green leaves and produces trumpet-shaped white flowers with lilac veins, in early summer.

• *CULTIVATION* Plant in autumn or spring in ordinary, well-drained soil and position in full sun or partial shade. Cut off the spent flower stems to encourage a second flush later in the season. Clumps can be divided either in autumn or spring.

• *PESTS AND DISEASES* Usually trouble free.

. . . .

GEUM

Rosaceae

Geum *chiloense* has many varieties, as well as modern hybrids. The following all form small, neat clumps 22-45cm (9-18in) high with a spread of 22-38cm (9-15in) and are suitable for the easy border. 'Lady Stratheden' has yellow flowers, 'Mrs J. Bradshaw' has red flowers, those of 'Fire Opal' are semi-double and flame-red. Also recommended are *G. borisii*, which has deep orange flowers, and *G. rivale*, the Water Avens, which has dark red calyces and yellow and pink flowers. *G. rivale* 'Leonard' is a good variety with copper-gold flowers. Both *G. borisii* and *G. rivale* flower in late spring,

GEUM BORISII

COUNTY LIBRARY

the others in early to midsummer. Geums can be short-lived plants.

• CULTIVATION   Geum likes some leaf mould added to any ordinary garden soil and can be planted in spring or autumn, in sun or partial shade. They can be fed if necessary with a general-purpose fertiliser. Sometimes the stems need supporting with twigs. If they increase they should be lifted and divided every few years, and they can be raised from seed.
• PESTS AND DISEASES   Usually trouble free.

HELLEBORUS

Ranunculaceae

Of the many species of helle-bores, the best low growing ones are Helleborus niger, the Christmas Rose, and H. orientalis, the Lenten Rose. There are several varieties of the former, and many of the latter, which cross-fertilises freely, producing seedlings of many colours. Both species have large, evergreen leaves reaching a height of 30-45cm (12-18in) and spreading to 30-45cm (12-18in), and are delightful plants.

H.niger, reputed to be one of the oldest cultivated plants, is said to have been introduced by the Romans. 'Niger' refers to its black roots, and the name hellebore comes from the Greek words 'hellein' to destroy, and 'bora', meaning pasture, as it was thought at one time to be harmful to grassland. The roots were also dried and ground and used rather like snuff as cures for headaches and melancholy. Protect its buds with a cloche to prevent them being spoilt by rain and bad weather, and you may be lucky enough to get the beautiful waxy white flowers at Christmas time.

Cut off the old leaves of H. orientalis in spring as the flower stems appear; this not only makes it easier to see and enjoy the flowers, but gets rid of the leaves which may be looking rather untidy after the winter; new leaves will emerge soon after. Flower colours range from green through pinks and reds to dark maroon. If you do not want seedlings, cut off the dead heads before they set seed.

• CULTIVATION Plant in autumn in good soil, with added leaf mould. They prefer moist soil and semi-shade. H. niger dislikes disturbance, taking time to get established. Allow 30-45cm (12-18in) between plants. Divide the clumps of H. orientalis in spring if necessary.
• PESTS AND DISEASES   Hellebores can be attacked by aphids in spring and the leaves may be affected by leaf spot. If this happens, spray with a combined insecticide/fungicide.
• BONUS POINTS   One of the few herbaceous plants to retain its leaves in winter.

HEUCHERA

Saxifragaceae
CORAL FLOWER

Hybrids of Heuchera sanguinea (syn. H. x brizoides) are the most commonly grown, and are suitable for the front of the easy border. They form clumps of evergreen leaves 25-30cm (10-12in) wide from which rise stems 30-45cm (12-18in) high, in early summer bearing tiny, coral-red flowers. Also available are H. 'Palace Purple' – purple-brown leaves and white flowers, H. 'Pearl Drops' – white flowers and H. 'Scintillation' – pink flowers.

• CULTIVATION   Plant either in spring or autumn in light, well-drained soil. Feeding is not usually necessary. The crowns tend to rise out of the soil, but this can be rectified by applying a mulch, or it is quite easy to lift and divide the clumps every few years which prevents this from happening.
• PESTS AND DISEASES   Usually trouble free.
• BONUS POINTS   The flowers are charming in small and medium-size arrangements.

HOSTA

syn. Funkia
Liliaceae
PLANTAIN LILY

There is a large number of species, and inumerable varieties and hybrids, of these popular plants, but I would advise planting only the small ones in the easy border. The large varieties can make huge clumps, and lifting and dividing them is a major undertaking. Digging them up requires considerable strength, and having done this it is usually necessary to cut up the clumps with a saw. The smaller varieties, however, can be more easily managed, especially if you do not pamper them and give them too rich a soil. They thrive in good, moist soil, in sun, partial shade, or shade. Some of mine have been put in full sun and left to their own devices and have rewarded me by remaining neat and manageable.

Buy plants from a reputable nursery which will advise you on which of the small varieties are suitable. They will include H. 'Blue Moon' with blue-green leaves, a spread of 30cm (12in) and mauve flowers on stems 12-20cm (6-8in) high. Among the medium-sized ones are H. lancifolia with dark green leaves and dark

HEUCHERA 'PALACE PURPLE'

• *PESTS AND DISEASES* The main problem with hostas is slugs and snails. If you have these in any number in your garden you will have to take drastic action as they will undoubtedly feast on the leaves. Resident hedgehogs are welcome as slug and snail predators. Slug pellets that are safe for dogs, birds and wild animals can be used, slug-and-snail traps containing beer will help to reduce their numbers, and a ring of coarse gravel or soot around a plant will often discourage them. They can cause considerable damage in some areas; if you have this problem I advise against including Hostas in your border. Apart from this the plants are usually trouble free.

• *BONUS POINTS* Hostas not only provide a large range of leaves of all forms and variegations, popular with flower arrangers, they also produce charming white or mauve flowers in midsummer. These much underrated flowers are excellent for cutting.

INCARVILLEA
Bignoniaceae
CHINESE TRUMPET FLOWER

*I*ncarvillea is named after the Jesuit priest, Pierre le Cheron d'Incarville, who collected plants in China during the eighteenth century. *I. delavayi* commemorates Abbé Jean Marie Delavay a French missionary and plant collector in China. It is one of my most favourite plants, producing strong stems with trumpet-shaped flowers of bright pink, in early to midsummer. It grows to between 45 and 60cm (18-24in) high with a spread of 30cm (12in) and has attractive fern-like leaves. There is also *I. mairei* which is very similar, but not so tall at 30cm (12in) high.

purple flowers, *H.* 'Weihenstephan', which has pale green leaves and white flowers, *H. undulata*, which has dark green leaves with white or cream markings, and *H. alba* with green leaves and white flowers. These have an average spread of 60cm (24in) and flower stems of 45cm (18in).

• *CULTIVATION* Hostas can be planted in either spring or autumn, and usually prefer rich, moisture-retentive soil, to which leaf mould or compost has been added. Some will tolerate wet, but most prefer reasonably well-drained soil. The variegated varieties keep the colour of their leaves better in partial shade. If you do not wish the plants to grow too vigorously choose a site in full sun with less rich soil, however they will not enjoy being kept too dry.

INCARVILLEA DELAVAYI

The plants die down completely in the winter. Be sure to mark their position with a strong label as it is very easy to catch their long roots with a hoe or fork when clearing up the border in the spring. The flower stems tend to appear before the leaves.

• *CULTIVATION* Plant in spring in a sunny position, in good rich soil that is well-drained. Allow 30cm (12in) between plants. A light mulch in autumn helps protect the plant in hard winters. Well-established plants can survive extremely low temperatures. Feeding is not usually necessary, but a general-purpose fertiliser, or blood, fish and bone, can be applied in the spring. It is a very neat-growing plant, and I have never had to move mine. Dividing it is almost impossible, but it is very easy to grow from seed. Do not put out young plants until they are really well established, this may be two or three years old if you live in a cold area.
• *PESTS AND DISEASES* Trouble free.
• *BONUS POINTS* A star performer for the easy border. It also produces

very fine seed heads, which are attractive when the flowers have faded. I cut most of these off after a few weeks, but leave one or two to set seed.

. . . .

❧ *LIATRIS* ❧

Compositae
BLAZING STAR
GAYFEATHER

*L*iatris spicata is another star performer, being neat-growing and requiring no staking. It produces spikes of bright pink flowers resembling bottle brushes in late summer. They are 45-60cm (18-24in) in height with a spread of 30cm (12in). There are now red and purple forms available, such as *L. s.* 'Kobold', as well as the white *L. s.* 'Alba'.

• *CULTIVATION* Plant in autumn or spring. *L. spicata* likes good, moisture-retentive soil, and will often tolerate being planted in bog gardens. Allow 30-45cm (12-18in) between plants. A mulch of compost or well-rotted manure is appreciated in the spring. The clumps can be lifted and divided as necessary.

• *PESTS AND DISEASES* Young shoots may be attractive to slugs, but otherwise it is trouble free.
• *BONUS POINTS* Being late in flowering, *Liatris* provides welcome colour in the border in late summer. The flowers also dry well. Pick them before they become fluffy and hang up to dry in a warm room.

. . . .

❧ *LIMONIUM* ❧

Plumbaginaceae

*L*imonium latifolium, syn. *L. platyphyllum*, has a rosette of large leaves 30cm (12in) across. The rosettes produce stems 30-40cm (12-16in) high bearing sprays of tiny lilac flowers in mid- to late summer.

• *CULTIVATION* Plant in spring, 30-40cm (12-15in) apart, in well-drained, ordinary soil in a sunny position. Feeding is not usually necessary. Can be grown from seed (see p.28).
• *PESTS AND DISEASES* Usually trouble free.
• *BONUS POINTS* *Limonium* dries well. Pick when the flower heads are opening and hang to dry.

. . . .

❧ *LYCHNIS* ❧

Carophyllaceae
JOVE FLOWER

*L*ychnis flos-jovis is a cultivated relation of the wild Campion. The flowers, which appear in early summer, are reddish-purple. 'Hort's Variety' has pink flowers. The leaves are silvery-grey. Height 45-60cm (18-24in) and spread 45cm (18in).

• *CULTIVATION* Plant in autumn or spring in ordinary, well-drained soil. It will tolerate a semi-shaded

LIATRIS SPICATA 'KOBOLD'

position. Allow 40cm (15in) between plants. To limit self sowing, cut off flowerheads before they set seed.

• *PESTS AND DISEASES* Usually trouble free, although aphids can attack the plant.

. . . .

୬! *LYSIMACHIA* !୭
Primulaceae
LOOSESTRIFE

All *Lysimachias* are invasive, with the exception of *Lysimachia ephemerum* which is neat-growing, and has grey leaves set on the stems of the flower spikes. The star-shaped, greyish-white flowers, which are sometimes tinged with mauve, appear in midsummer. They are long lasting. The plant, which spreads to 30cm (12in), may need some support as it can reach 1m (3ft) in height.

LIMONIUM LATIFOLIUM 'BLUE CLOUD'

• *CULTIVATION* Plant in good soil in autumn or spring, in a sunny or partially shaded position. Allow 40cm (15in) between plants. Feeding is not usually necessary. Divide the clumps and replant in autumn or spring.

• *PESTS AND DISEASES* Trouble free.

• *BONUS POINTS* A welcome tall plant for the back of the border, the grey leaves are attractive.

❧ *LYTHRUM* ❧

Lythracea

PURPLE LOOSESTRIFE

There are two good varieties of *Lythrum salicaria*. 'Robert' bears spikes, 75cm (30in) high, of bright magenta-pink, four-petalled flowers in late summer. It spreads to 45cm (18in). 'Firecandle' has rose-pink flowers and is similar to 'Robert' but taller, the spikes reaching 60-90cm (24-36in). *L. virgatum* varieties, 'Rose Queen', which is pink, and 'The Rocket', which is deep pink, are similar to the *L. salicaria* varieties, and are also recommended.

• *CULTIVATION* *Lythrum* can be planted in ordinary soil in sunny positions, but also does well in bog gardens. Allow 45-60cm (18-24in) between plants. Feeding is not usually necessary. The roots can be divided in spring or autumn.

• *PESTS AND DISEASES* Trouble free.

• *BONUS POINTS* *Lythrum* do not require staking and, therefore, are useful at the back of the border. They provide welcome colour at the end of the season.

. . . .

MORINA

Morinaceae

Morina longifolia is a most striking and unusual plant. Some years ago a friend gave me seed from which I raised three seedlings; I have been delighted with them. The thistle-like leaves form an extremely neat clump, 30cm (12in) across, and produce, in midsummer, prickly spikes, 60-75cm (24-30in) high, bearing tiny white flowers that gradually turn pink.

• *CULTIVATION* Plant in good, well-drained soil in a sunny position. Allow 30-45cm (12-18in) between plants. Feeding is not usually needed. It is wise to protect the dormant plants in winter with a mulch of peat or bracken. They produce long tap roots, which do not like disturbance, but they can be grown from seed if required.

• *PESTS AND DISEASES* Usually trouble free.

• *BONUS POINTS* Visitors to your garden will be impressed with this plant. If you pick the heads for drying, do this before the tiny flowers fade and hang the stalks upside down in a warm room.

. . . .

PENSTEMON

Scrophulariaceae

These plants, because they are not always fully hardy, really belong in the Borderline Directory, this being their only fault, and because they are so very delightful and popular, I have included them in

MORINA LONGIFOLIA

this list. Because of their reputation I did not grow them for many years, but I have been surprised and pleased to find that, with just one exception, they have survived in my garden through the last few winters. However, as we have not had really severe winters for some years, it may well be that I have been lucky. If you are prepared to face possible losses, they are easily replaced either by buying new or by taking cuttings in late summer.

Although there are quite a few species, most of the freely available penstemons are hybrids and varieties. There is a good range of colours available, from white, to pink, red and purple. They are free flowering, with long-lasting blooms from mid- to late summer, require no staking, and are generally a delight in the border. They grow to about 45-60cm (18-24in) in height with a spread of 45-60cm (18-24in).

I recommend buying from a reliable nursery, which will advise you on those that are suitable for your area; these may include P. 'King George', with salmon red flowers, P. 'Schoenholzeri' (syn. 'Ruby'), with ruby-red flowers, P. 'Garnet' (syn. 'Andenken an Friedrich Hahn'), with wine-red flowers, the white P. 'Snowstorm' and the pink, red-throated P. 'Apple Blossom'.

• *CULTIVATION* Plant in spring, in ordinary, well-drained soil, in a sunny position. Allow 45-60cm (18-24in) between plants. Cut them back almost to the base in spring; leaving the spent foliage on the plants over winter helps to protect them from cold. Take cuttings in late summer and keep in a well-protected cold frame or greenhouse through the winter. Harden off before planting out in spring, when all danger of frost has passed.
• *PESTS AND DISEASES* Trouble free.
• *BONUS POINTS* Penstemons will provide colour for many weeks in the garden and do not need staking.

❧ PLATYCODON ❧
Campanulaceae
BALLOON FLOWER

*P*latycodon grandiflorus is a neat-growing plant producing 30-60cm (12-24in) stems bearing bluish-purple, bell-shaped flowers in midsummer. The variety *P.g. mariesii*, height 30-45cm (12-18in), is an especially good form and there is also the white variety *P.g. albus*. They all have a spread of 30-45cm (12-18in).

PENSTEMON 'APPLE BLOSSOM'

• *CULTIVATION* Plant in autumn or late winter in well-drained soil and a sunny position. Allow 38cm (15in) between plants. Feeding is not usually necessary. Divide and replant old clumps, or grow from seed. Prick out the seedlings before the fleshy roots have formed, and plant in their permanent positions. The fleshy roots dislike disturbance, so may take some time to settle down. Be sure to mark their position well; as with *Incarvillea* it is all too easy to damage the roots when weeding in the spring before the flower stems emerge.

• *PESTS AND DISEASES* Usually trouble free.

. . . .

❧ POLEMONIUM ❧

Polemoniaceae

JACOB'S LADDER

*P*olemonium foliosissimum, unlike its relative *P. caeruleum*, does not set seed and can be classed as easy. In form it resembles the latter, but the leaves are dark green, and the cup-shaped flowers are mauve-blue. It flowers in summer, grows 75cm (30in) high and 60cm (24in) across and should not require staking.

I christened *P. caeruleum* 'Pandemonium' because seedlings appeared everywhere in my border; it has now been banned.

───────────

• *CULTIVATION* Plant in autumn or spring in a sunny or partially shaded position. Although tolerant of poor soil, it will do much better if given a generous helping of well-rotted manure, or compost, when set out. Allow 45cm (18in) between plants. Not always long lived, it may need lifting and dividing every few years and can be raised easily from seed.

• *PESTS AND DISEASES* Trouble free.

. . . .

POTENTILLA 'GLOIRE DE NANCY'

❧ POTENTILLA ❧

Rosaceae

CINQUEFOIL

*P*otentillas are delightful plants, flowering profusely, and lasting for many weeks. They are similar in appearance to *Geum*. There are several species of herbaceous potentilla; one of the best is *Potentilla rupestris*, which produces 45cm (18in) stems bearing white, saucer-shaped flowers, with yellow centres, in early summer.

Cultivars of *P. nepalensis* include the pink 'Miss Willmott', and 'Roxana', which is orange-red. There are also many *Potentilla* hybrids. One of the most striking is the semi-double *P.* 'Gloire de Nancy', with orange and dark red flowers, others include *P.* 'Gibson's Scarlet', with bright scarlet flowers, the dark red *P.* 'Flamenco', and *P.* 'Yellow Queen', which has flowers of yellow and red.

The flower stems of all these grow to between 45 and 60cm (18-24in) in height, and they flower in mid-summer. They form a neat clump of leaves 45cm (18in) across, but the stems tend to flop over, and will require some support if you want them to remain neat. If they are positioned next to a more erect, sturdy neighbour this will help keep them under control, otherwise a few twigs or a herbaceous support are helpful.

───────────

• *CULTIVATION* Plant either in spring or autumn in ordinary, well-drained garden soil, in a sunny position. Allow 30-45cm (12-18in) between plants. Mulch with well-rotted compost in spring. Divide long-lived clumps in spring, or raise new plants from seed.

• *PESTS AND DISEASES* Trouble free.

. . . .

PRIMULA VULGARIS AND HELLEBORUS ORIENTALIS

❧ PRIMULA ❧
Primulaceae

*P*rimula auricula is one of the oldest cottage-garden plants. It was introduced to Britain in the sixteenth century and during the nineteenth century was popular as florist's flowers, raised for the show-bench by weavers and workmen. The ones recommended for the easy border are the modern hybrids, which are fully hardy, and produce polyanthus-like heads of many colours in spring. Left to themselves they produce large clumps, 15-23cm (6-9in) high and 15-20cm (6-8in) across, of pale green leaves, and only require division when the clumps exceed their allotted space. They are excellent for the front of the border, and require nothing more than to have their dead heads removed after flowering. They can be raised from seed if necessary.

P. vulgaris is the common Primrose, and this and its many new garden hybrids are all excellent for the front of the border, as long as the soil has plenty of humus and is moisture-retentive, but does not get too wet. Care is needed in hot summers as the plants dry out quickly. I try to place mine so that a herbaceous neighbour partly shades them in summer. They grow 15-20cm (6-8in) in height and spread. Divide any clumps that have grown too large after flowering, and put the offsets in a nursery bed. These can be planted out in autumn.

P. denticulata produces drumstick-like heads of flowers in spring. These can be pink, lilac, purple or white with a height of 15-30cm (6-12in). The clumps increase in size each year but do not need dividing for several years if enough space is allowed.

They are very easy plants and one of the first spring flowers to appear.

• *CULTIVATION* Auriculas like ordinary soil which is well-drained, but has had plenty of well-rotted manure or compost, and some organic fertiliser, worked into it. They can be placed in a sunny or partially-shaded position. *P. vulgaris* and *P. denticulata* prefer soil that is rich in leaf mould or humus, and are best planted, 20-30cm (8-12in) apart, in the autumn. Lift and divide as necessary after flowering.

• *PESTS AND DISEASES* *P. denticulata* and Auriculas have always been trouble free in my garden, but Primroses can be affected by various types of rot. If a plant is obviously not doing well, throw it away, and replace with new stock.

• *BONUS POINTS* Primulas are one of the first flowers of spring, and provide colour for many weeks. They go well with Wallflowers and bulbs in a spring bedding scheme.

❧ PULSATILLA ❧
Ranunculaceae

*P*ulsatilla vulgaris, the Pasque flower, is so called because it flowers at Easter time in Britain – indeed the leaves were used at one time to dye Easter eggs. It is a delightful plant, forming a neat clump of feathery leaves, 15-23cm (6-9in) across, with reddish-purple cup-shaped flowers. Suitable for the front of the border, it is now available in several shades of pink and red.

P. alpina subsp. *apiifolia* (syn. *P.a.* subsp. *sulphurea*) has white flowers, and is 15-30cm (6-12in) high with a spread of 10-15cm (4-6in).

• *CULTIVATION* Plant in late summer in a sunny position, in well-drained soil that contains plenty of humus.

Allow 20cm (8in) between plants. They can be grown from seed.
• *PESTS AND DISEASES* Usually trouble free.
• *BONUS POINTS* The flowers form attractive seedheads which are very long lasting.

. . . .

❧ *RANUNCULUS* ❧
Ranunculaceae
BUTTERCUP

*R*anunculus aconitifolius 'Flore Ple-no' (Fair Maids of France) is an early flowering plant, producing in

late spring, small, double, white flowers on stems 45-60cm (18-24in) high. It is slightly lax spreading to 50cm (20in), but does not need staking. The species has been grown in cottage gardens since Elizabethan times. It was introduced from France, hence its common name.

———

• *CULTIVATION* R.a. 'Flore Pleno' likes good moist soil, which does not dry out, and it can be grown in bog gardens. Sun or partial shade is preferred.
• *PESTS AND DISEASES* Trouble free.

RANUNCULUS ACONITIFOLIUS 'FLORE PLENO'

❧ *SALVIA* ❧
Labiatae/Lamiaceae

*M*ost of the herbaceous salvias are half-hardy, but *Salvia nemorosa* (syn. *S. virgata* var. *nemerosa*) 'East Friesland', which grows to 75cm (30in), and 'Lubecca', which grows to 45cm (18in), are fully hardy. They form neat clumps 45cm (18in) across and produce spikes bearing small tubular, violet-blue flowers in mid- to late summer.

———

• *CULTIVATION* Plant either in autumn or spring in a sunny position, in well-drained soil to which has been added well-rotted manure or compost. Allow 30-38cm (12-15cm) between plants. Divide the clumps in autumn or spring.
• *PESTS AND DISEASES* Usually trouble free.

. . . .

❧ *SAXIFRAGA* ❧
Saxifragaceae

*S*axifraga x urbium is one of the oldest cottage-garden plants. Originally the common name London Pride was given to *S. umbrosa*, which was grown extensively in London gardens although it is thought by some to have been named after George London, royal gardener to William III. The hybrid of *S. umbrosa* and *S. spathularis* is now most usually grown, with its rosettes of dark green leaves and 30cm (12in) stems bearing tiny pink flowers in early summer. The plants continue to spread if left unchecked, but it is very easy to pull off any unwanted portions. It is advisable to renew the clumps by replanting these and throwing away the older parts of the plant every few years.

• *CULTIVATION* *Saxifraga* x *urbium* likes well-drained soil with added grit, and limestone chippings, if available, and a sunny or partially-shaded position. Allow 45cm (18in) between plants. Feeding is not necessary.

• *BONUS POINTS* Usually trouble free.

❧ *SCABIOSA* ❧
Dipsacaceae

There are many varieties of *Scabiosa caucasica*, which was introduced from the Caucasus mountains in the nineteenth century and became a favourite cottage-garden plant. The name is derived from 'scabies', meaning itch, as some of the species were supposed to cure this irritation.

The most common-grown varieties are 'Clive Greaves', which has mauve flowers, 'Moerheim Blue', with violet-blue flowers, the light blue 'Moonstone', and the white 'Miss Willmott'. They make neat rosettes of leaves 60cm (24in) wide from which grow stems, 60cm (24in) tall, bearing flowers from mid- to late summer. The stems, which are a little lax, can flop over, but if sited next to a strong neighbour, they will do no harm. There are also charming short-stemmed varieties called *S.* 'Blue Butterfly' and *S.* 'Pink Mist', height and spread 20-30cm (8-12in), they've blue and pink flowers respectively.

S. rumelica (syn. *Knautia macedonia*) produces small, dark red flowers, which resemble pincushions, from early to late summer and forms a neat clump 75cm (30in) high and 60cm (24in) across. It does require support.

• *CULTIVATION* Plant *Scabious* in spring 30-45cm (12-18in) apart in good rich, well-drained garden soil.

They like a sunny position and do not usually need feeding. They can be divided every three or four years.

• *PESTS AND DISEASES* Slugs and snails can attack early growth and mildew can affect the leaves.

• *BONUS POINTS* *Scabious* are excellent as cut flowers. Cut off the dead heads to ensure a good supply of blooms.

❧ *SEDUM* ❧
Crassulaceae

Sedum 'Autumn Joy' is very neat-growing, with pale green leaves spreading to 45cm (18in). It produces stems 45cm (18in) tall, with flowerheads appearing in late summer. The flowers are pink at first, turning to orange and then brown and are very attractive to butterflies. *S. spectabile* 'Brilliant' has rose-pink flowers. *S.* 'Ruby Glow' has purple-green leaves and forms a rather lax clump 20-30cm (8-12in) across. The flower stems topped with maroon flowers grow to 25cm (10in) in height. The clumps increase slowly and can be lifted and divided quite easily.

• *CULTIVATION* Plant in ordinary, well-drained soil in a sunny position in either spring or autumn. Allow 30-40cm (12-16in) between plants. Feeding is not necessary.

• *PESTS AND DISEASES* Slugs can attack new leaves and stems, and the roots may become rotten if the soil is too wet.

• *BONUS POINTS* If picked when the heads are well formed, and before they turn brown, they keep quite well for a few months. Hang the stems upside down in a warm room to dry.

SCABIOSA CAUCASICA 'CLIVE GREAVES'

SEDUM 'AUTUMN JOY'

SMILACINA

Liliaceae

FALSE SPIKENARD

Smilacina racemosa is a delightful plant. Unlike Solomon's Seal (*Polygonatum*), to which it is related, it is not invasive. In late spring or early summer it produces long lasting, creamy-white flowerheads, on stems 60-75cm (24-30in) tall. It spreads to about 75cm (30in) across.

• *CULTIVATION* Smilacina likes good, moist soil, and semi-shade. Mine was planted on the edge of my bog garden, in full sun, and has been perfectly happy there, requiring no attention. Allow 50cm (20in) between plants. Lift and divide old plants in the autumn.

• *PESTS AND DISEASES* Trouble free.

• *BONUS POINTS* The flowers are scented.

SOLIDAGO

Compositae

GOLDEN ROD

Solidago canadensis was introduced by John Tradescant the younger, in the middle of the seventeenth century. It is one of the old cottage-garden plants, but for the easy border the shorter new garden hybrids are recommended. The colours range from pale to bright yellow. They will not grow too tall and do not require support. I have a charming one called 'Lena' which grows from 30 to 45cm (12-18in) high and forms a small clump 15-20cm (6-8in) across. It dries beautifully, but may now be unobtainable. There are others, including 'Golden Baby' (syn. 'Gold-kind'), 60cm (24in) high, and 'Queenie' (syn. 'Golden Thumb'), 30cm (12in) high. Also recommended is 'Lemore', 60cm (24in), which is now classified under x *Solidaster luteus*. They all make neat clumps 20-30cm (8-12in) across.

• *CULTIVATION* Plant 25cm (10in) apart in ordinary garden soil in spring or summer in sun or partial shade. Feeding is not usually necessary. The clumps can be divided and replanted, when necessary, in the autumn or spring.

• *PESTS AND DISEASES* Usually trouble free, but the leaves can be affected with powdery mildew. Spray with a fungicide if this occurs.

• *BONUS POINTS* Golden Rod blooms in late summer and is excellent as a cut flower. It also dries well; cut when about half the flowerhead is open, strip off the leaves, bunch and hang to dry in a warm room.

. . . .

❧ STACHYS ❧

Labiatae

There are several species of *Stachys*, but the best for the easy border is *S. macrantha*. It makes neat clumps 30-45cm (12-18in) high and 30-60cm (12-24in) across. The leaves are wrinkled and the whorls of purple flowers are carried in midsummer. A good variety is 'Superba', with purple flowers. 'Rosea', with pink flowers and 'Violacea', which has violet flowers, are obtainable from some nurseries.

• *CULTIVATION* Plant between autumn and spring in ordinary, well-drained soil in a sunny or partially-shaded position. Feeding is not usually necessary. Divide old clumps in autumn or spring, and allow 40cm (16in) between plants.

• *PESTS AND DISEASES* Trouble free.

. . . .

❧ TRILLIUM ❧

Liliaceae/Trilliaceae
WOOD LILIES

There are several species of these charming plants, the leaves and flowers of which are formed in three parts, hence their name; 'tri' meaning three. Formerly classed as lilies, they may still be found listed in bulb catalogues. They are very expensive, so be sure to mark their position carefully with a strong label to avoid damaging them when they are dormant. The lovely three-petalled flowers, which appear in the spring, are well worth the money.

Among the species that are available are *Trillium erectum*, which has purple-red flowers and grows 30cm (12in) high, *T. grandiflorum*, the Wake Robin, growing to 30-45cm (12-18in) with white flowers that turn pink, and *T. sessile*, which has marbled leaves and dark red flowers and is 15-30cm (6-12in) tall. They all spread from 20-38cm (8-15in) across.

• *CULTIVATION* *Trillium* likes moist soil that contains plenty of humus, but which is well-drained. Although they prefer partial shade, mine are quite happy in full sun on the edge of my bog garden. Allow

SMILACINA RACEMOSA

25-30cm (10-12in) between plants. Very large clumps can be lifted and divided in late summer, or in mild weather during the winter, but the replanted young portions will take time to get established. They are very difficult to raise from seed.

• *PESTS AND DISEASES* Trouble free, though slugs may attack young shoots.

❧ TROLLIUS ❧

Rancunculaceae
GLOBE FLOWER

There are several species of Trollius. *T. europaeus* has been grown in gardens since the sixteenth century. The name is believed to have come from the Scandinavian 'troll' meaning a witch, as at one time it was thought that the plant had supernatural powers.

The modern hybrids of *T. x cultorum* provide a greater range of colours than the yellow of *T. europaeus*. These include 'Canary Bird', which is lemon-yellow, 'Orange Princess', which is orange-yellow, and 'Salamander', which is bright orange. They are all delightful plants, forming neat clumps 45cm (18in) across and producing large 'buttercup' heads, on stems 30-45cm (12-18in)

tall, in late spring or early summer.

• *CULTIVATION* Plant in ordinary garden soil, which does not dry out, in spring or autumn. Allow 30-38cm (12-15in) between plants. Water well in dry weather. Feeding is not usually necessary. If the dead heads are removed after flowering, a second flush of blooms may sometimes appear in late summer. Old clumps can be divided as necessary.

• *PESTS AND DISEASES* Usually trouble free.

• *BONUS POINTS* Clumps of *Trollius* increase in size slowly, and need only be lifted and divided if they outgrow their allotted space.

❧ VERATRUM ❧

Liliaceae/Melanthiaceae
FALSE HELLEBORE

Veratrum *album* and *nigrum* are unusual and handsome plants. The leaves resemble those of the *Hosta*, and make a neat clump 60cm (24in) across. Tall, strong stems, 1-1.2m (3-4ft) tall, bear small flowers which are either white or black, according to the variety, from mid- to late summer.

• *CULTIVATION* *Veratrum* likes good, moist soil, and should be planted in spring or autumn in a slightly shaded position. Allow 60cm (24in) between plants. Feeding is not usually necessary. Large clumps can be divided in autumn or early spring.

• *PESTS AND DISEASES* Usually trouble free, although slugs can attack the emerging leaves.

• *BONUS POINTS* The heads of *V. nigrum* will dry if picked when fully open and hung upside down in warm room.

VERATRUM NIGRUM

VERONICA

Scrophulariaceae

SPEEDWELL

Probably the best species of *Veronica* for the easy border is *spicata*. This forms neat clumps of foliage, 45cm (18in) across, which in early summer produce 30-45cm (12-18in) tall stems bearing racemes of tiny bright blue flowers. The variety 'Red Fox' (syn. 'Rotfuchs') flowers in late summer, and has shorter stems, 20-25cm (8-10in) high, of pinky-red flowers. *V.s.* 'Alba' is a white variety. There are also other cultivars of *V. spicata* available with pink or violet-blue flowers. The flower stems do sometimes flop, and a small herbaceous support or a few twigs will help to keep the clump tidy. 'Red Fox' does not require staking.

V. gentianoides is a charming plant for the front of the border. It makes a mat of leaves 45cm (18in) across which, in late spring, produce 20-30cm (8-12in) stems bearing pale blue flowers. A variety with variegated green and white leaves is also available. It does not require support.

• *CULTIVATION* Veronicas like good soil, to which some well-rotted manure or compost has been added. Full sun or partial shade suits them. Plants should be set out 40cm (16in) apart. Feeding is not necessary. If the clumps outgrow their allotted space, lift and divide them. This can be a little difficult with *V. spicata* as the clumps are very dense and hard, so a sharp spade and a strong arm are helpful. 'Red Fox' and *V. gentianoides* are very easy to divide.

• *PESTS AND DISEASES* Mine have always been trouble free, but they can be attacked by powdery mildew. If this occurs, spray with a fungicide.

• *BONUS POINTS* Excellent for cutting.

. . . .

VERONICA GENTIANOIDES

DIRECTORY OF BORDERLINE PERENNIALS

The plants listed here will need more attention than those described in the main Directory. Some require lifting and dividing every few years, others will need staking, but none are invasive or otherwise badly behaved. If you have the time, and energy, and are willing to provide this extra attention, these 'borderline' plants are well worth a place in your garden.

ACHILLEA 'MOONSHINE'

❧ *ACHILLEA* ❧

Compositae

YARROW

The large Achilleas have no place in the easy border; they require staking and the clumps regularly need lifting and dividing, the strong, deep roots making this is a very difficult task.

The smaller *Achillea taygetea* can be classed as borderline, although this may have to be divided every three years. It has heads of pale lemon-yellow flowers on stems 45cm (18in) high in midsummer, and grey leaves. It spreads to 60cm (24in).

A. 'Moonshine' which is slightly taller at 60cm (24in) high, has bright at heads of yellow flowers and grey leaves.

_____

• *CULTIVATION* Plant in autumn or spring in well-drained soil in a sunny position and allow 45cm (18in) between plants. Feeding is not necessary. Lift and divide the clumps when they exceed their allotted space.

• *PESTS AND DISEASES* Usually trouble free.

• *BONUS POINTS* The flowerheads will dry if picked when fully formed and ripe and before they discolour. Strip off the leaves and hang up to dry.

∙ ∙ ∙ ∙ ∙ ∙ ∙ ∙ ∙ ∙ ∙ ∙ ∙ ∙ ∙ ∙ ∙ ∙ ∙ ∙

❧ AGAPANTHUS ❧
Liliaceae
AFRICAN LILY

Agapanthus praecox subsp. orientalis (syn. A. orientalis) is half hardy, and forms a clump 60cm (24in) across of strap-shaped leaves. In midsummer it produces strong stems 60-90cm (24-36in) in height, bearing umbels of blue flowers. If you live in a mild area you will be able to grow these handsome and long lived flowers. The 'Headbourne Hybrids' are more hardy, and with some protection may well survive in colder areas.

• CULTIVATION Plant the crowns in spring, 5cm (2in) below ground level, in good, well-drained, fertile soil, in a sunny position. Protect the plants with bracken in winter if they are likely to suffer frost damage. Allow 45cm (18in) between plants. Feeding is not usually necessary. The clumps increase slowly, but may have to be lifted and divided eventually.
• PESTS AND DISEASES Usually trouble free.

. . . .

AGAPANTHUS 'HEADBOURNE HYBRIDS'

❧ AQUILEGIA ❧
Ranunculaceae
COLUMBINE

There are reputed to be a hundred species of Aquilegia, but the most commonly known one is A. vulgaris and its many garden hybrids. The Granny's Bonnet, or Granny's Mutch is a British wild flower. It has blue flowers, but white and double forms have been developed. Both common names refer to the shape of the flowers. The modern hybrids have larger flowers than A. vulgaris, and some, like the pink-and-green 'Nora Barlow' are double. Heights vary from 15 to 90cm (12-36in) and although they do not need staking, the stems can be toppled by gales or heavy rain.

There are shorter types available, such as the 'Music Series Hybrids' and 'Dragonfly', and these would be more suitable for the easy border. However, a word of warning, Aquilegias seed themselves with great abandon, so be sure to remove the dead heads in good time.

• CULTIVATION Plant out in the spring in good, well-drained soil, either in full sun or partial shade. Set out 20cm (8in) apart. Feeding is not necessary. Propagation is no problem, as they self-sow.
• PESTS AND DISEASES The list of diseases Aquilegias may suffer from includes gall mite, downy mildew, mosaic virus, club root and white blister, but I have never had any trouble with them in my garden.

. . . .

❧ ASTER ❧
Compositae
MICHAELMAS DAISY
STARWORT

There are over 500 species of perennial Aster. They are most charming but do suffer from various

ASTER AMELLUS 'KING GEORGE'

diseases. Powdery mildew is the most common, and is not only very difficult to control, but ruins the appearance of the plants. *A. novi-belgii* and *A. novae-angliae* need to be lifted and divided regularly, so they are not included in this Directory. However, *A. amellus*, which is a native of Italy and the true Starwort, is worth including for its daisy-like flowers in autumn. With a height and spread of 50cm (20in), the most well known cultivar is 'King George' which has violet-blue flowers; there is also a pink form, 'Lady Hindlip'. I have never had any trouble with these plants, but in my northern garden plants are seldom attacked by mildew.

A delightful species is *A. ericoides*. This flowers very late in the season and has tiny white flowers, which are very long lasting. It was one of Gertrude Jekyll's favourite plants and

it is clear why she was so fond of it. My plant, given to me by an old lady who did not know what it was, grows to 45-60cm (18-24in) and never needs staking. Some cultivars are not so upright in habit as mine, so if you buy one make sure it does not have lax growth and that the stems stand up well.

You may like to try *A. thompsonii* 'Nanus', which grows to 45cm (18in) high, with a spread of 25cm (10in), and has large, lavender-blue flowers and grey-green leaves.

• *CULTIVATION* Plant in autumn or spring in good, well-drained soil in a sunny position, 25cm (10in) apart. Feed with general-purpose fertiliser or blood, fish and bone, in the spring. Divide the clumps as necessary.
• *PESTS AND DISEASES* Many and various! Should you find mildew a

problem I recommend removal.
• *BONUS POINTS* Asters are excellent as cut flowers.

. . . .

❧ *ASTILBE* ❧
Saxifragaceae

There are two reasons why these delightful plants are not included in the main Directory: they need constantly moist soil and they are difficult to lift and divide when they outgrow their allotted space. If you can provide the moisture-retentive soil they demand, for instance, in a bog garden or near a pool, and allow plenty of room for them to increase in size, they will be little trouble. However, the time will come when you will have to lift and divide them, retaining only the outer, younger portions of the plant. As with large Hostas, digging them up requires considerable strength and you will have to chop into the roots with a sharp spade, or even use a saw. There is a large range of both species and hybrids available, with summer flowers in every colour from white through to dark red. They grow from 30 to 90cm (12-36in) in height and spread according to type.

• *CULTIVATION* Plant in moisture-retentive soil in sun or partial shade, in autumn or spring. Allow 30-40cm (12-18in) between plants. Apply a mulch of well-rotted compost, leaf mould or peat in early spring. Lift and divide clumps every three years.
• *PESTS AND DISEASES* Usually trouble free.
• *BONUS POINTS* The pink and dark red flowers dry well if picked before they become too fluffy. Hang them upside down in a warm room. Also excellent for flower arranging.

. . . .

❦ BERGENIA ❧
Saxifragaceae
ELEPHANT'S EARS

There are several species of *Bergenia*, but most of the plants on sale are modern hybrids. The racemes of cup-shaped flowers, produced in spring, range in colour from white to pink, red, and dark red. The large, almost round leaves vary in colour from green to maroon and purple. Among the best are: 'Silberlicht', which is 30-38cm (12-15in) high and has white flowers shading to pink; 'Abendglut', 23cm (9in) high and rosy-red; and 'Bressingham White' 30cm (12in). Although they are often used as groundcover and can spread to 90cm (36in) or more, they increase slowly, and as long as you give them plenty of room, they are very easy plants, particularly the small varieties.

• *CULTIVATION* Plant in any ordinary soil in autumn or spring. They will tolerate partial shade. Allow 30cm (12in) between plants. Feeding is not necessary. When the time comes to restrict their growth, pull up the thick stems, and replant only the rooted young, outer portions.
• *PESTS AND DISEASES* Usually trouble free, but brown blotches on the leaves denote leaf spot fungus. This is often caused by lack of nutrients. Remove all the infected leaves, spray with a fungicide, and apply some general-purpose fertiliser. Remove all dead leaves in spring.
• *BONUS POINTS* The leaves are excellent for flower arrangements.

ASTILBE HYBRID

❦ CAMPANULA ❧
Campanulaceae
BELL FLOWER

Campanula lactiflora is a lovely plant for the back of the border, but as it can grow up to 1.2-1.5m (4-5ft) in height, it usually requires staking. If you are prepared to provide this, using a strong herbaceous support, I highly recommend it for the easy border. The lavender-blue, bell-shaped flowers in midsummer are charming, and there is also a pink variety 'Loddon Anna'. Both spread to 60cm (24in).

C. latifolia grows to 1.2m (4ft)

and, in my garden, has never required staking. However, it does have a reputation for seeding itself, so be sure to cut off the heads in good time. It has flowers of blue-purple; a white form is also available.

• *CULTIVATION* Plant in autumn or spring in good garden soil, and in a sunny position. Allow 45cm (18in) between plants. Feeding is not usually necessary. Clumps can be lifted and divided.
• *PESTS AND DISEASES* Usually trouble free, though slugs and

CAMPANULA LATIFOLIA

snails can attack the young shoots, and rust may sometimes develop on the leaves.
• *BONUS POINTS* These tall campanulas are useful for the back of the border.

· · · · · · · · · · · · · · · ·

❧ *DIANTHUS* ❧
Caryophyllaceae
GARDEN PINKS

*P*inks are so well known they hardly need describing. They are in this Directory as they are so popular, and no border would be complete without them, but they are not altogether trouble free. Their main fault is that they need to be propagated regularly; the old plants become woody and eventually die. If you are prepared to either take cuttings or to buy new plants as necessary they are a delight. Most of them have a delicious scent and are excellent as cut flowers.

There are too many *Dianthus* to list; the choice is endless. There are the old-fashioned pinks with single varieties such as 'Charles Musgrave', white flowers with a green eye, and 'Brympton Red', white and red flowers, to the double 'Dad's Favourite', with white flowers laced with purple, and 'Mrs Sinkins', simply white. Then there are the modern garden pinks, developed from *D. plumarius* and the dwarf Highland hybrids. Both types are between 25 and 38cm (10-15in) high and spread to about 23-30cm (9-12in) across. They flower in mid- to late summer, sometimes with a second flush in autumn.

D. caryophyllus is the old clove pink with purple flowers in mid- to late summer. Named by the Greeks in honour of Jove, it was used to make coronets, hence the word 'car-nation' derived from 'coronation'. The plant is thought by some to have been introduced into Britain on stones, imported for building castles by William the Conqueror. The old name 'Gillyflower' is probably a corruption of 'July flower' although many *Dianthus* flower earlier. Clove Pink reaches 23cm (9in) high and may be up to 45cm (18in) across.

It is easy to become addicted to these delightful flowers; there is a wide range available from most good garden centres, and the rarer species, varieties and hybrids can be obtained from specialist nurseries.

────────

• *CULTIVATION* *Dianthus* like a sunny position, in well-drained soil that has had well-rotted manure or compost worked into the base of the planting hole. Although they like good drainage, they can suffer from lack of water, but certainly do not like heavy, wet soil. Spring planting is best; work some bonemeal into the soil before setting the plants out. Add lime if the pH is below 6.5. Allow 25cm (10in) between plants. Feeding is not usually necessary, but a foliar feed, high in potash, can be applied if required. Always cut stems down to the base when the flowers are over, and remove straggly or unhealthy growth at any time. Young plants may need the growing tips pinched out to encourage bushy growth. Cuttings can be taken in summer. Put these in small pots containing a mixture of sharp sand and compost, and place in a shaded cold frame. When rooted they can be planted out in mild areas, or overwintered in a cold frame in colder regions.
• *PESTS AND DISEASES* These plants are very tempting to pigeons and pheasants. Whole plants may be stripped in the winter. I now

DIANTHUS 'HIGHLAND HYBRIDS'

protect mine with wire netting. Border carnations often recover from these attacks, but pinks are usually killed. Diseases which can affect the plants include rust, fusarium wilt, rot and mildew.

• *BONUS POINTS* Both Pinks and Border Carnations are excellent as cut flowers.

. . . .

❧ *DICENTRA* ☙

Papaveraceae

BLEEDING HEART
DUTCHMAN'S TROUSERS

*D*icentra spectabilis forms a neat clump of ferny foliage 75cm (30in) high with a spread of 50cm (20in), with heart-shaped pink-and-white flowers in early summer. *D. s. alba* has white flowers. Both are

charming plants, but tend to die down after flowering, and can thus leave a gap in the bed or border. Place them so that a neighbouring plant covers this gap.

———————

• *CULTIVATION* Plant in spring or autumn in good soil, adding leaf mould or compost, and lime if your soil is at all acid. Allow 50cm (20in) between plants. Feeding is not usually necessary. Divide and replant as necessary.

• *PESTS AND DISEASES* Usually trouble free, although they resent disturbance once established.

• *BONUS POINTS* Small children love the flowers, which, when gently opened, resemble a ballerina, or 'lady in the bath'.

DICTAMNUS

Rutaceae

BURNING BUSH

*D*ictamnus albus is known as the 'Burning Bush' because it is supposed to be possible to ignite the volatile oils given off by the plant by holding a match to the flowers on a still, warm evening. I have never tried this experiment so cannot vouch for the truth of the common name.

The plant is very slow growing, hates disturbance and cannot be divided, and it will be several years before flowers are produced. It is also wise to provide support because it has a very slender neck, which can be snapped off by high winds. Despite these drawbacks I am assured by my most trusted expert that it is a charming and worthwhile plant and well worth trying. *D. albus* grows to 60cm (24in) with a spread of 60cm (24in), flowers in mid-summer and has white flowers and dark green leaves; *D. albus* var. *purpureus* has pink flowers, striped with red.

• *CULTIVATION* Plant in autumn or spring in well-drained soil, to which lime should be added, 50-115gm/sq. m (2-4oz per sq. yd), if your soil is acid. Allow 45cm (18in) between plants. New or extra plants will have to be raised

from seed, or purchased.

• *PESTS AND DISEASES* Usually trouble free.

GAILLARDIA

Compositae

BLANKET FLOWER

*T*he *Gaillardia* hybrids come in various colours from dark red to yellow, orange and brown, and combinations of these colours. They grow from 60 to 75cm (24-30in) high with a spread of 30-40cm (12-16in), flowering in summer and usually needing some support. They are rather short-lived plants but are well worth trying in warmer areas.

• *CULTIVATION* They like light, well-drained soil, and a sunny position. Plant in spring. They are easily grown from seed. Allow 40cm (16in) between plants. Cut off spent flowerheads to encourage more blooms. Feeding not usually necessary.

• *PESTS AND DISEASES* Usually trouble free, but downy mildew can attack the leaves.

• *BONUS POINTS* Excellent as cut flowers. Remove the dead heads to encourage more blooms.

GILLENIA

Rosaceae

*G*illenia trifoliata has wiry, red stems, and produces small, five-petalled white flowers in midsummer. It can grow to 1-1.2m (3-4ft) in height with a spread of 60cm (24in), and may require staking, but if you are prepared to provide this it can be useful in the back of the border.

• *CULTIVATION* Plant between autumn and spring in ordinary soil in a sunny or partially-shaded position. The clumps, which should

GILLENIA TRIFOLIATA

be placed 50-60cm (20-24in) apart, are neat growing. Feeding is not usually necessary. Divide and replant clumps as necessary.

• *PESTS AND DISEASES* Usually trouble free.

• *BONUS POINTS* A useful tall plant for the back of the border.

. . . .

❧ *HOSTA* ✣

syn. *Funkia*

Liliaceae

PLANTAIN LILY

(see main Directory for cultural details)

There is a very large selection of Hostas; the smaller ones, which are suitable for the easy border are listed in the main Directory (p.76). Most nurseries have a good range of plants on sale, and specialist nurseries provide even more of the varieties available.

The larger Hostas make very hard root balls, so if you wish to enjoy these handsome plants you must be prepared to allow plenty of room around them, and when they outgrow this space you will need a pair of very strong arms, a sharp spade and a small saw to lift and divide them! If you suffer from slugs and snails in your garden, I would not recommend Hostas.

. . . .

❧ *LINUM* ✣

Linaceae

FLAX

Linum narbonense, which grows from 30 to 60cm (12-24in) high and spreads to 30-45cm (12-18in), produces a flush of bright blue five-petalled flowers every morning from early summer until autumn. Sadly, it is not entirely hardy, or long lived, but it is very easy to grow from seed.

• *CULTIVATION* Plant 30cm (12in)

apart in well-drained soil, in a sunny position. Feeding is not usually necessary. Propagate from seed.

• *PESTS AND DISEASES* Usually trouble free.

• *BONUS POINTS* The seedheads are useful for dried flower arrangements. Pick before the pods open, and hang up to dry in a warm room.

· · · · · · · · · · · · · · · · · ·

❧ LYCHNIS ❧
Caryophyllaceae

Lychnis *chalcedonica*, Jerusalem Cross, is supposed to have been brought back by the Crusaders. The small, scarlet Maltese-cross-shaped flowers are held in tight bunches on 60-90cm (24-36in) high stems in early summer. It requires support, but is otherwise an easy plant.

―――――――――――

• *CULTIVATION* Plant 30-38cm (12-15in) apart in autumn or spring in ordinary, well-drained soil in a sunny or partially-shaded position. A mulch of well-rotted manure or compost is helpful each spring. Clumps can be lifted and divided as necessary.

• *PESTS AND DISEASES* Usually trouble free, but can be attacked by a virus which causes mottling of the leaves.

• *BONUS POINTS* Very few herbaceous plants produce scarlet flowers, *L. chalcedonica* is popular for doing so.

· · · · · · · · · · · · · · · · · ·

LYCHNIS CHALCEDONICA

❧ MONARDA ❧
Labiatae
BEE BALM
BERGAMOT
OSWEGO TEA

Monarda *didyma* was named for a Dr. Monardes of Seville in the sixteenth century. Its common name comes from the resemblance of the scent to the bergamot orange, and it has long been a cottage-garden plant. All parts of it have a strong citrus smell and can be used for perfume and pot pourri. Bergamot has whorls of red, pink or white flowers from early to late summer. The leaves are made into herbal teas. It is useful for the back of the border, growing from 60 to 90cm (24-36in) tall and 45-75cm (18-30in) across. It may require support.

―――――――――――

• *CULTIVATION* In spring or autumn, plant several Bergamots in a group, 10cm (4in) apart in good, moisture-retaining soil. Mulch with well-rotted manure or compost each spring. It can be slightly invasive, but the roots are easy to pull up. It should be divided every few years, replanting only the young, outer portions which have good roots. Keep well watered in dry weather.

• *PESTS AND DISEASES* Usually trouble free.

• *BONUS POINTS* A useful plant for the back of the border.

· · · · · · · · · · · · · · · · · ·

❧ NEPETA ❧
Labiatae
CATMINT

Nepeta x *faasenii* with its pale lavender-blue flowers in early summer, is such a popular plant that I think it must be included in this Directory. However, it is not always trouble free – it dies in wet, cold winters, and if you own cats they will

MONARDA DIDYMA

lie and roll on it and you will be left with a *Nepeta prostrata!* A few sharp twigs inserted into the clump may dissuade them from indulging in this irritating habit. It also flops and although it is attractive spilling on to a paved path, you will be left with a bald patch if it falls over on to a grass path. Growing from 30 to 45cm (12-18in) high and spreading to 60cm (24in) it can be classed as borderline. The taller varieties are best avoided.

• *CULTIVATION* Nepeta will grow happily in sandy or stony soil, even in chalk, but it dislikes heavy, poorly-drained soil. New plants should be set out in the spring. Allow 30cm (12in) between them. It is best to cut the dead foliage away in spring; remove the spent flower stems in the summer to encourage a second flush. Divide and replant as necessary.
• *PESTS AND DISEASES* Usually trouble free, but the leaves can be attacked by powdery mildew.
• *BONUS POINTS* Sweet smelling, Catmint is popular with both flower arrangers and cats!

❧ PAEONIA ❧
Paeoniaceae
PEONY

There are more than ten species of this lovely flower, which the Greeks named in honour of Paian, the god of healing, and made use of the roots in the treatment of various ailments. I would dearly like to have been able to include some of them in the main Directory, but they are not always the easiest of plants, and all of them require support. The best known are *P. officinalis*, which is an old cottage-garden plant, and the modern varieties of *P. lactiflora*.

Paeonies dislike disturbance, and can take some years to get established, but when they do well they are splendid border plants. Heights range from 60 to 90cm (24-36in) and they can spread up to 90cm (36in). The foliage is attractive long after the flowers have faded. The flowerheads, which appear in early summer, are large and heavy, and they, as well as the foliage, do require support, having to be tied in regularly as the plants grow, which can be very time consuming.

• *CULTIVATION* Paeonies like well-drained, but moisture-retentive soil, in a sunny or partly-shaded position. Plant 60-92cm (24-36in) apart, in autumn or spring. Use plenty of well-rotted manure or compost when planting, and do not place the crowns more than 2.5cm (1in) below the surface. Feed with bonemeal, and apply this, and a mulch, each year. Crowns can be divided, and portions with roots replanted.
• *PESTS AND DISEASES* These include paeony wilt, grey mould and physiological disorders.
• *BONUS POINTS* The foliage is useful for flower arranging throughout the summer.

❧ PHLOX ❧
Polemoniaceae

There are several species of this lovely old cottage-garden plant, but sadly they can be attacked by several diseases and are very prone to infestation by eelworm. *Phlox maculata*, however, seems to be resistant to this pest and is worth trying. Like all phlox it has a wonderful scent; the flowers of the species, which bloom in mid- to late summer, are purple. Two forms, 'Omega', white flowers with lilac centres, and 'Alpha', with pink flowers, are also available. They grow to 60-90cm (24-36in) in height with a spread of 75cm (30in) but do not usually require staking.

• *CULTIVATION* Plant in autumn or spring in a sunny or partially-shaded position, in good well-drained soil. Allow 45cm

SIDALCEA 'OBERON'

(18in) between plants. An annual mulch of well-rotted manure or compost is beneficial. Lift and divide the clumps every 2-3 years, using only the young, outer portions for replanting.

• *PESTS AND DISEASES* Include powdery mildew, leaf gall and spot.

. . . .

❧ *SIDALCEA* ❧
Malvaceae

*I*f you are prepared to give sidalceas a herbaceous support they are easy and attractive plants. Their hollyhock-like flowers are borne from mid- to late summer. Many of the modern varieties are descended from *Sidalcea malvaeflora* and include 'Croftway Red', deep red flowers, 'Loveliness', shell-pink flowers, 'Oberon', with rose-pink flowers, and 'William Smith', with salmon-pink flowers. Their height varies from 75 to 90cm (30-36in) with a spread of 45cm (18in) or more.

———

• *CULTIVATION* Plant in autumn or spring in ordinary garden soil, 45cm (18in) apart. Feeding is not usually necessary. In milder areas cut down to 30cm (12in) after flowering as you may get a second set of lateral shoots and blooms. If the clumps get too large or cease to produce good blooms, they will need to be lifted and divided, retaining only the outer, young portions for replanting.
• *PESTS AND DISEASES* Usually trouble free, though the leaves can be attacked by rust.
• *BONUS POINTS* Useful for the back of the border.

. . . .

❧ *SISYRINCHIUM* ❧
Iridaceae

*S*isyrinchium striatum is semi-perennial and grows to 60cm (24in) in height with a similar spread. It produces creamy-white trumpet-shaped flowers, striped with purple, in early to midsummer. The smaller *Sisyrinchium* species seed themselves everywhere, and have been banned from my garden, but *S. striatum* is much easier to control and is very handsome. Remove the fading flowerheads if you do not want it to self-sow.

———

• *CULTIVATION* Plant in a sunny position, 25-30cm (10-12in) apart, anytime from autumn to spring, in well-drained soil, to which leaf mould or peat has been added.
• *PESTS AND DISEASES* Usually trouble free.

. . . .

TANACETUM COCCINEUM 'BRENDA'

❧ TANACETUM ❧

syn. *Pyrethrum*

Compositae/Asteraceae

The Pyrethrum Daisies, *Tanacetum coccineum,* are very easy plants, but do require staking and, in time, will require dividing, which is not easy, as they eventually make very hard, dense clumps 45cm (18in) or more across. Any weeds, such as couch grass, which do manage to get into the clumps, will have to be removed by using a weed glove. (See Weed Control, p.26.) The daisy-like flowers are borne on stems 60-90cm (24-36in) high in early summer, and are excellent for cutting. Good varieties include 'Brenda', deep pink flowers, and 'Bressingham Red', crimson flowers. There are also double varieties available. The flower stems will need staking, a herbaceous support put in place early in the spring is the best way to stop them flopping over.

• *CULTIVATION* Plant in autumn or spring in good, well-drained soil, in a sunny position, 40-45cm (16-18in) apart. Feeding is not usually necessary. Cut off all flower stems as soon as they have faded, to encourage a second flush of blooms. Divide every 3-4 years, using the outer, young portions for replanting.

• *PESTS AND DISEASES* Usually trouble free.

• *BONUS POINTS* Excellent as cut flowers.

DIRECTORY OF SHRUBS

Note: Although heights have been given for the following shrubs, these may vary greatly. Two *Salix* (Willows) in my garden, both of which are supposed to grow only 1m (3ft) tall, are already well over 2m (6ft) and still growing; at the other end of the scale, most *Euonymus* are reputed to be able to reach 3m (10ft) in height, but in my garden they have always remained well below 1m (3ft). Thus heights are approximate and will depend on area, climate, soil and pruning.

BALLOTA

Labiat'ae/Lamiaceae

Ballota acetabulosa and *B. pseudodictamnus* are deciduous sub-shrubs, and both are suitable for either the mixed or herbaceous border. They have woolly grey-green leaves, and whorls of tiny white flowers in midsummer. They make neat bushes 60cm (24in) tall with a spread of up to 1m (3ft).

- *CULTIVATION* *Ballota* tolerates poor soil, and likes a sunny position. Plant in the spring. Established plants should be cut back by half each spring.
- *PESTS AND DISEASES* Usually trouble free.
- *BONUS POINTS* Dries well. Pick before the tiny flowers turn brown and hang up to dry in a warm room.

CARYOPTERIS

Verbenaceae

Caryopteris x *clandonensis*, which is deciduous, forms a bush 60cm-1.2m (2-4ft) in both height and spread. It produces bright blue flowers in late summer. Good varieties are 'Heavenly Blue', 'Kew Blue' and 'Arthur Simmonds', which all make very neat bushes.

- *CULTIVATION* *Caryopteris* does well

CARYOPTERIS × CLANDONENSIS 'ARTHUR SIMMONDS'

in ordinary soil in a sunny position. Plant in autumn or spring. Cut out all weak growth in spring and reduce strong stems by half. It is not entirely hardy so the protection of a wall is helpful.

- *PESTS AND DISEASES* Trouble free.

DAPHNE

Thymelaeaceae

There are several species of *Daphne*, but probably the best known one is the deciduous, winter-flowering *D. mezereum*, which has clusters of purple or pink blooms. Although it can grow to 1.5m (5ft) it seldom reaches this height, and certainly not in colder areas, where it will require the protection of a wall. It can be temperamental, dying for no apparent reason, but is well worth trying.

Daphne tangutica Retusa group, which is slow growing, has an eventual height and spread of 60-90cm (24-36in). It is a charming shrub, and makes a neat bush of glossy evergreen leaves, with purple buds opening in clusters of pinky-white flowers in late spring.

• *CULTIVATION* Plant in autumn or spring in ordinary, well-drained soil, to which some chalk has been added. Position in a sunny or partially shaded position.
• *PESTS AND DISEASES* Daphnes can be attacked by aphids, cucumber mosaic virus and leaf spot.
• *BONUS POINTS* Deliciously scented flowers.

. . . .

❧ DEUTZIA ❧
Philadelphaceae

There are several species of *Deutzia*, but most are rather large. The best for the easy mixed border is *D. x rosea* 'Carmina', with a height and spread 90cm (3ft). It is a deciduous shrub, which has clusters of rose-pink flowers in summer. The variety 'Campanulata' has white flowers.

• *CULTIVATION* Plant between autumn and late winter in ordinary, well-drained soil, in either a sunny or slightly shady position.
• *PESTS AND DISEASES* Usually trouble free.

. . . .

FUCHSIA MAGELLANICA
VAR. *GRACILIS*

❧ EUONYMUS ❧
Celastraceae

The varieties of *Euonymos fortunei* are excellent for the mixed border. Although they can grow up to 2.5-3m (8-10ft) with a spread of up to 2m (6ft) they seldom reach this height as the evergreen, variegated foliage is much in demand by flower arrangers, and frequent cutting keeps the shrubs neat and compact. The many varieties available include: 'Emerald 'n' Gold', with green and yellow leaves; 'Emerald Gaiety', with leaves of green and white; 'Gold Tip',

with cream and green leaves; the green and white 'Silver Queen'; and 'Sunspot', green leaves with a yellow centre

• *CULTIVATION* In colder areas *Euonymus* will welcome the protection of a wall, or should be placed in a sheltered part of the garden. Plant them in the autumn or spring, in ordinary garden soil in sun or partial shade.

• *PESTS AND DISEASES* Usually trouble free.

• *BONUS POINTS* Variegated *Euonymus* provide coloured foliage all the year as well as valuable material for flower arranging.

✿ FUCHSIA ✿

Onagraceae

Some of the hybrid Fuchsias are hardy, and can be included in the

mixed bed. A reputable nursery will advise you on those that are suitable, and they will include 'Alice Hoffman', red-and-white flowers, height and spread 75cm (30in), and 'Display' with pink flowers and growing to a height of 1m (3ft) and a spread of 75cm (30in). 'Lady Thumb', red-and-pink flowers and 'Tom Thumb', red-and-purple flowers, both reach 50cm (20in) in height and spread.

A charming species is *F. magellanica* var. *gracilis* which has pink-tinged, green leaves, and dainty crimson-and-purple flowers from midsummer to autumn. It can reach 2.2m (7ft) heigh with a spread of up to 1.2m (4ft), but in cold areas will not grow more than 1-1.2m (3-4ft).

• *CULTIVATION* Fuchsias like well-drained soil, to which has been added humus in the form of leaf mould or peat. Add some bonemeal to the soil when planting. In colder areas they may die down in the winter; the dead stems should be cut away in spring.
• *PESTS AND DISEASES* Usually trouble free.

❧ *GAULTHERIA* ❧
syn. *Pernettya*
Ericaceae

*G*aultheria mucronata is a small evergreen shrub with a height and spread of 60-90cm (24-36in), which can get rather untidy eventually. If this happens cut it back hard in spring. It produces small white flowers in spring and early summer, followed by berries in the autumn. There are several named forms, which include 'Alba', which has white berries; 'Rosea', pink berries; and 'Bell's Seedling', cherry-red berries. Most books recommend planting several to assist pollination.

• *CULTIVATION* Plant anytime between late summer and early spring, though obviously not in very cold, frosty weather. *Gaultheria* like lime-free soil, but will tolerate ordinary soil if plenty of peat is worked in around their roots when they are set out. Mine has done well in rather poor soil.
• *PESTS AND DISEASES* Usually trouble free.

❧ *HEBE* ❧
Scrophulariaceae

*H*ebes are among my most favourite plants. The ones listed are all well behaved, hardy and evergreen. Flowering in the summer, with attractive leaves and spikes of flowers, they are both decorative and useful in the mixed bed or border.

H. albicans is neat growing, 60cm (24in) in both height and spread, although it can grow larger; trim it regularly to keep it compact. It produces white flowers in early to midsummer. *H. armstrongii* 'Autumn Glory' is hardy, given some protection, and grows to 60-90cm (24-36in). It produces violet-purple flowers from late summer into the autumn. *H. pinguifolia* 'Pagei' has grey-green leaves, and produces small white flowers in early summer. Height 20-24cm (8-10in). It can

HEBE ALBICANS

spread to over 1m (3ft), but is easily cut back. *H.* 'Rosie' is a new hybrid with pink flowers from early summer. It is compact and 30cm (12in) high with a spread of 60cm (24in). If you live in a mild area, try the charming *H. macrantha*, which produces beautiful white flowers in early summer.

- *CULTIVATION* Hebes can be planted in any well-drained soil, in spring or autumn.
- *PESTS AND DISEASES* Usually trouble free.
- *BONUS POINTS* The foliage of Hebes is useful for flower arranging throughout the year.

❧ *HELICHRYSUM* ❧

Compositae

CURRY PLANT

*H*elichrysum italicum (syn. *H. augustifolium*) is an evergreen sub-shrub with aromatic silver-grey leaves that smell strongly of curry. It forms a small bush 60cm (24in) in height with a spread of 75cm (30in). Clusters of small mustard-yellow flowers are borne in midsummer.

- *CULTIVATION* *H. italicum* likes a sunny position and sharply drained soil. Allow 45cm (18in) between plants. It is not entirely hardy.
- *PESTS AND DISEASES* Usually trouble free, but downy mildew can attack the leaves.

❧ *PHILADELPHUS* ❧

Hydrangeaceae

*P*hiladelphus microphyllus is a compact, deciduous small shrub, which produces very fragrant, four-petalled, white flowers in summer. It grows to 60-90cm (24-36in) high and wide. There are also many hybrids, but most of them are too

PHILADELPHUS MICROPHYLLUS

large for the easy mixed border.

- *CULTIVATION* Plant from autumn to early spring in ordinary, well-drained soil, in a sunny or partially-shaded position.
- *PESTS AND DISEASES* Usually trouble free.

❧ *POTENTILLA* ❧

Rosaceae

(Herbaceous Potentillas are listed in the main Directory, p.83)

*T*he deciduous Potentillas are my most favourite shrub, and every

year I add to my collection. Entirely trouble free and flowering throughout the summer, they are a joy to behold – the perfect subject for the mixed bed or border. There are several species and innumerable hybrids so you can get them in almost every colour. Height and spread vary, from 60cm to 1.2m (2-4ft), but they can be kept neat by clipping them every spring and removing some older branches if these become untidy.

Some of my favourites include cultivars of *P. fruticosa*: 'Abbotswood', white flowers; 'Daydawn', creamy-

POTENTILLA 'PRIMROSE BEAUTY'

yellow flowers, 'Elizabeth', bright yellow flowers; 'Princess', pink flowers; 'Red Ace', bright red flowers; 'Royal Flush', pink flowers fading to white; the deep orange 'Sunset'; and 'Tilford Cream', creamy-white flowers.

• *CULTIVATION* Plant in autumn or spring, in well-drained soil in full sun. Some shade is tolerated, but they will not flower so profusely.
• *PESTS AND DISEASES* Trouble free.
• *BONUS POINTS* Potentillas are unsurpassed for ease of maintenance and continuous flowering.

. . . .

🌿 RUTA 🌿
Rutaceae
RUE

*R*uta graveolens is an evergreen herb with a very bitter flavour. It makes a neat bush 30-60cm (12-24in) in height and spread. The clusters of tiny yellow flowers are borne in early to midsummer. The leaves are greyish-blue. 'Jackman's Blue' is compact with brighter foliage. Sap from the stems can act as an irritant. It is advisable to wear gloves when handling the foliage, particularly when picking it in bright daylight (see box p.62.)

• *CULTIVATION* Plant in autumn or spring, in ordinary well-drained soil in a sunny position. Prune back the foliage to old wood in spring, and remove the flowerheads in autumn.
• *PESTS AND DISEASES* Trouble free.
• *BONUS POINTS* The foliage of rue is useful for flower arranging, but has a rather unpleasant smell.

. . . .

SANTOLINA
🌿   🌿
Compositae/Asteraceae
COTTON LAVENDER

*S*antolina chamaecyparissus (syn. *S. incana*) makes a neat bush

45-60cm (18-24in) in height and spread. The leaves are aromatic, and evergreen, but usually get damaged in winter. Bright yellow flowers, like small buttons, are produced in midsummer.

• *CULTIVATION* Plant in either autumn or spring, in any ordinary well-drained soil, in a sunny position. The weight of the flower stems can cause the bush to open up and become untidy; prevent this from happening by either removing the stems after flowering, or by using a herbaceous support in early spring. Cut the bush back in the spring, if necessary to keep it neat, or if the leaves have been damaged in the winter.
• *PESTS AND DISEASES* Usually trouble free.
• *BONUS POINTS* The foliage is excellent for flower arranging; the flowers will dry if picked in good condition and hung in a warm room.

. . . .

🌿 SKIMMIA 🌿
Rutaceae

*S*kimmia japonica is an evergreen shrub, which grows from 1 to 1.5m (3-5ft) in height. It forms a neat bush 1-1.2m (3-4ft) across, and has dense cluster of white flowers in the spring. Both male and female bushes are necessary to produce berries. For example, 'Fructu-albo' (female) with 'Fragrans' (male). Regular removal of foliage for flower arranging will help keep the bush to a manageable size. The variety 'Rubella' has red-rimmed foliage and red flowers.

S. japonica subsp. *reevsiana* is not quite so dense and compact, but is slower growing. It produces creamy-white flowers in spring followed by red berries.

• *CULTIVATION* Plant in autumn or spring, in ordinary garden soil in either sun or partial shade.
• *PESTS AND DISEASES* The leaves can become yellow, which denotes chlorosis; this may be caused by too much sun or poor soil. Apply a solution of sequestrene if this happens. A mulch of leaf mould and compost in spring is helpful.
• *BONUS POINTS* The foliage is invaluable for flower arranging.

. . . .

🌿 VIBURNUM 🌿
Caprifoliaceae
GUELDER ROSE

*V*iburnum carlesii is a deciduous shrub 1-1.2m (3-4ft) in height and spread, and produces gloriously sweet-smelling, pinky-white flowers in early spring.

V. opulus 'Compactum' grows up to 1.5m (5ft) and has deep green leaves, which turn red in the autumn. In the spring it produces ball-headed white flowers followed by bright red berries.

There are many different species and hybrids of *Viburnum*, but most of them are too large for the easy border. A little careful pruning will keep these two shrubs to a manageable size. Both are deciduous.

• *CULTIVATION* Plant *V. carlesii* in good garden soil, which does not dry out, between mid-autumn and early spring. Choose a reasonably sheltered position, to protect the flowers from frost. *V. opulus* 'Compactum' flowers later so frost should not be a problem.
• *PESTS AND DISEASES* Can be attacked by aphids, but otherwise usually trouble free.
• *BONUS POINTS* *V. carlesii* is one of the most deliciously scented of all spring shrubs.

. . . .

DIRECTORY OF BULBS

❧ *ALLIUM* ❧
Liliaceae/Alliaceae

Only *Allium aflatunense*, height 75cm (30in), and *A. giganteum*, height 1m (3ft), are recommended for the easy border, although there are more than a dozen species of Alliums, and they range in height from a few centimetres to several metres tall. The smaller ones tend to increase rapidly, and can become a little invasive.

The two listed are ideal, and are handsome, easily grown plants. They flower in early summer and produce large ball-shaped, red or purple flowerheads.

ALLIUM

• *CULTIVATION* Alliums like well-drained soil and a sunny position. Plant the bulbs in autumn, or spring, 7-10cm (3-4in) below the surface. After flowering, remove the dead heads, but not the leaves, which are needed to provide food for the bulb.

• *PESTS AND DISEASES* Usually trouble free.

• *BONUS POINTS* The seed heads will dry if picked before they are spoilt by wet weather.

❧ BRODIAEA ☙

Liliaceae/Alliaceae

Some years ago I bought a packet of *Brodiaea laxa* bulbs. I had never heard of them, but was taken by the illustration which showed clusters of upright, starry-shaped purple-blue flowers on 30-45cm (12-18in) stems. They have proved

BRODIAEA CORONARIA

one of my most rewarding impulse buys. In early summer they are a delight; long lasting and trouble free, they come at the end of the bulb season and are all the more welcome for being late arrivals. There are also other species of *Brodiaea* including *B. coronaria*, now classified under *Dichelostemma* and *Triteleia*, which may be suitable. Mark the position of the bulbs so you do not disturb them when the foliage has died down.

• *CULTIVATION* Plant the bulbs in early autumn in well-drained soil in a sunny site, preferably sheltered.

• *PESTS AND DISEASES* Trouble free.

❧ CAMASSIA ☙

Liliaceae/Hyacinthaceae

QUAMASH

There are several species of *Camassia*, the best known being

C. quamash. The name comes from the Indian word for this variety, which was used as food. The star-shaped flowers can be blue, white or purple, and appear in midsummer on stems 75cm (30in) tall. *C. leichtlinii*, is considered one of the best to grow, as it has strong, 1m (3ft) high stems.

• *CULTIVATION* Plant in good soil, which does not dry out, in the autumn. Set the bulbs 7-10cm (3-4in) deep. Remove the dead heads after flowering.

• *PESTS AND DISEASES* Usually trouble free.

❧ CYCLAMEN ☙

Primulaceae

The little hardy *Cyclamen* are a delight with their attractive, bright red, pink or white flowers. If you can find a small space for them in the front of the bed or border where the corms will not be disturbed they will reward you by being trouble free.

C. coum (syn. *C. ibericum, C. orbiculatum, C. vernum*) has 7cm (3in) high flowers in red, pink or white, from midwinter to early spring, and the leaves often have silvery markings. *C. purpurascens* has 10cm (4in) high red flowers from mid- to late summer, and leaves that are marbled with silver. *C. hederifolium* (syn. *C. neapolitanum*) produces 10cm (4in) high, mauve and pale pink flowers from midsummer to mid-autumn, and the silver- marked leaves last for many months. There is also a white variety, *C.h. album.* ·

• *CULTIVATION* Cyclamens like well-drained soil, which contains plenty of well-rotted compost, and a sheltered position, preferably shaded from hot sun; they can be planted under shrubs. Set them out singly or in groups of three, with the corms placed 15cm (6in) apart, and do not cover them too deeply with soil, especially *C. hederifolium.* An annual mulch of leaf-mould after the flowers are over is beneficial.

• *PESTS AND DISEASES* Usually trouble free, although the corms can be eaten by mice.

• *BONUS POINTS* Clumps of *Cyclamen* can increase, but the corms are easily lifted and replanted elsewhere. The leaves are much prized by flower arrangers.

ERYTHRONIUM
Liliaceae

*E*rythronium dens-canis, the Dog's Tooth Violet, with its pinky-purple six-petalled, reflexed flowers, 10-15cm (4-6in) high in spring, is perhaps rather small for the border, but the varieties of *E. revolutum,* which have stems 30-45cm (12-18in) high, make attractive clumps of white, pink or purple flowers in late spring or early summer. *E.* 'Pagoda' with yellow flowers, and *E. californicum* 'White Beauty' are two others you may like to try.

• *CULTIVATION* Erythroniums like to be planted deep in good, rich soil which does not dry out, in light shade. Although the roots are tuberous, the plants are often listed under 'Bulbs'. Set them out late summer, and leave undisturbed.

• *PESTS AND DISEASES* Usually trouble free.

FRITILLARIA
Liliaceae

*T*here are more than eighty species of *Fritillaria*, but perhaps the best known is *F. meleagris*, the Snake's Head Fritillary. This grows wild in some areas, but is more usually cultivated in gardens. The bell-like white flowers with purple markings appear in spring, hanging from stems 30-45cm (12-18in) high. There are several other forms including *F. m. alba*, with white flowers 30-45cm (12-18in) high.

Other species include *F. pallidiflora*, 30-38cm (12-15in), which has greenish-yellow flowers and *F. pontica*, 45cm (18in) high, which has green flowers.

F. imperialis, the Crown Imperial, is not included as it presents a problem in that having flowered in

ERYTHRONIUM DENS-CANIS

FRITILLARIA MELEAGRIS ALBA

early spring, it leaves a large gap in the border, which cannot easily be filled with another plant.

• *CULTIVATION* F. meleagris likes moist conditions, so do not plant the bulbs where they will dry out in the summer; the other varieties like well-drained soil and a sunny position. Plant the bulbs 10-15cm (4-6in) deep, and mark their position carefully to prevent disturbance once the leaves have died down.

• *PESTS AND DISEASES* Usually trouble free.

GALTONIA
Liliaceae/Hyacinthaceae
SUMMER HYACINTH

Galtonia candicans produces very lovely 1-1.2m (3-4ft) high, white flowers, very similar to a large Hyacinth, in mid- to late summer. The flowers are slightly scented.

• *CULTIVATION* Set the bulbs

between herbaceous plants in the border, at least 15cm (6in) deep in early spring, placing 3-5 together.
• *PESTS AND DISEASES* Usually trouble free, although grey mould can attack the bulbs.

GLADIOLUS
Iridaceae

Unlike the large *Gladiolus* hybrids, *G. byzantinus*, Sword-lily, can be left in the ground and does not need lifting in the autumn. The flowers, which are wine-red, appear in early summer and are carried on 45cm (18in) high stems. The corms are small, so it is advisable to mark their position to prevent accidentally digging them up when working on the bed.

• *CULTIVATION* Plant the corms in the autumn, 5-7cm (2-3in) deep, in well-drained soil, in a sunny position.
• *PESTS AND DISEASES* Usually trouble free.
• *BONUS POINTS* Excellent as cut flowers.

IRIS
Iridaceae

The Dutch Xiphium hybrid Irises are easily grown, and produce white, blue or purple flowers in midsummer. They are excellent as cut flowers, and make neat clumps 45cm (18in) high in the border.

• *CULTIVATION* Plant the bulbs in groups of 5-7, about 10-15cm (4-6in) deep, in the autumn. The bulbs increase every year, and the clumps will need lifting and dividing every 3-4 years. This is very easily done, and the extra bulbs can be replanted or, if not required, given away.

WHITE XIPHIUM IRIS

• *PESTS AND DISEASES* The bulbs can be attacked by mould, but I have never had any trouble with the ones in my garden.

• *BONUS POINTS* Each stem produces two flowerheads, the second one opening when the first has died.

🌿 *LEUCOJUM* 🌿
Liliaceae/Amaryllidaceae
SNOWFLAKE

*L*eucojum aestivum resembles a giant Snowdrop and produces its long lasting flowers in late spring. It can grow between 45 to 60cm (18-24in) in height. A clump of these bulbs in a bed or border a real delight.

• *CULTIVATION* Plant in clumps in late summer or early autumn, 8-10cm (3-4in) deep, 5-8cm (2-3in) apart in moisture-retaining soil, in a sunny or partially-shaded position. If the clumps get too large, lift and divide them.

• *PESTS AND DISEASES* Trouble free.

❧ NARCISSUS ❧

Liliaceae/Amaryllidaceae

DAFFODILS

In the easy border standard-sized Daffodils are not recommended, as the leaves, which should not be cut down for at least six weeks after flowering, flop and turn brown and leave gaps that cannot be filled later – altogether very unsightly. However, the miniature varieties, which are rightly becoming so popular, can be tucked into small spaces in the front of the border and are charming in the spring. Three that I grow are: *Narcissus* 'Tête-à-Tête', which is yellow and has several flowers on each stem; 'Minnow', which is pale yellow; and 'Hawera' which also bears several creamy-yellow flowers on each stem. Heights vary from 15 to 25cm (6-10in), and all flower in the spring. There are many more to choose from, but check their height. It is wise to mark their positions so that you do not disturb the bulbs when the leaves have died down.

• *CULTIVATION* Plant in groups in the autumn, setting the bulbs at the depth directed on the packet. They like good soil which is well-drained, and need plenty of sun in the summer to ripen the bulbs.

• *PESTS AND DISEASES* Usually trouble free.

❧ NERINE ❧

Liliaceae/Amaryllidaceae

Nerine bowdenii, the Guernsey Lily, is recommended for the easy border. There is a charming, but untrue, story of how these bulbs came to be called Guernsey Lilies, which states that the bulbs were washed ashore on the beach, after a ship returning from the Cape was wrecked off the island. They had, however, been discovered some time before this event.

N. bowdenii is hardy, and produces spherical heads of wavy-petalled, pink flowers in the autumn. 'Fenwick's Variety' has larger flowerheads of a deeper pink.

• *CULTIVATION* Plant either in midsummer, or in spring, in ordinary, well-drained soil, in a sunny position at a depth of 10cm (4in).

• *PESTS AND DISEASES* Usually trouble free.

• *BONUS POINTS* Flowering in the autumn, Nerines are a joy, providing welcome colour in the border late in the year. If you have enough of them, and can bear to pick them, they are wonderfully long lasting as cut flowers.

❧ TULIPA ❧

Liliaceae

The bulbs of T. kaufmanniana can be left in the ground to increase and naturalise and do not have to be lifted after flowering. They are best in a mixed bed or border where they can be allowed to spread. In the easy border they may become a little invasive.

Ordinary Tulips that have been grown in pots or containers can be replanted in the border after flowering and often do quite well in subsequent years. The secret is to plant them deeply, 20-25cm (8-10in) below the surface. Put them between clumps of perennials, and every spring you will be rewarded by their blooms, which make a nice splash of colour among emerging perennials.

• *CULTIVATION* T. kaufmanniana should be planted in late autumn, 10-15cm (4-6in) below the surface, and 5-8cm (2-3in) apart.

• *PESTS AND DISEASES* Usually trouble free, although all can be attacked by viruses and grey mould.

Pages 118–19
Solidago, agapanthus, nepeta and lythrum in the border at Oxburgh Hall, Norfolk.

Plant Lists

The plants listed in the following pages are recommended for your easy garden. A word of caution is necessary, however if mistakes are to be avoided: **Make sure you buy the variety or species listed,** for example – Anaphalis triplinervis is clump-forming but A. yeodensis is invasive.

❧ PLANTS LISTED IN THE MAIN DIRECTORY ❧

Aconitum.	*A.* 'BRESSINGHAM SPIRE', *A.* x *cammarum* var. *bicolor, A. compactum* 'CARNEUM', *A.* 'IVORINE', *A. napellus, A.* 'NEWRY BLUE'
Anaphalis.	*A. triplinervis*
Armeria.	*A. pseudoarmeria* 'BEES HYBRIDS'
Aurina.	*A. saxatilis* (syn. *Alyssum saxatile*), *A. s.* 'FLORE PLENO', *A. s.* var. *citrina, A. s.* 'VARIEGATA'
Brunnera	*B. macrophylla*
Carlina.	*C. acaulis caulescens*
Celmisia.	*C. coriacea*
Cirsium.	*C. japonicum*
Coreopsis.	*C. verticillata*
Diascia.	*D. rigescens, D. vigilis* (syn. *D. elegans*)
Dierama.	*D. pendulum* and varieties, *D. pulcherrimum* and varieties
Doronicum.	*D. austriacum, D. cordatum* (syn. *D. columnae*), *D.* x *excelsum* 'HARPUR CREWE', *D.* x *e.* 'MISS MASON'
Dodecatheon.	Species
Echinacea.	*E. purpurea* (syn. *Rudbeckia purpurea*), *E. p.* 'ROBERT BLOOM', *E. p.* 'WHITE LUSTRE'
Erigeron.	Hybrids including 'DIGNITY', 'DUNKELSTE ALLER' (syn. 'DARKEST OF ALL'), 'FELICITY', 'PROSPERITY', 'QUAKERESS'
Eryngium.	*E. variifolium*
Euphorbia.	*E. polychroma*
Filipendula.	*F. vulgaris* (syn. *F. hexapetala*), *F. v.* 'FLORE PLENA'
Gentiana.	*G. asclepiadea*
Geranium.	*G. renardii*
Geum.	*G. borisii, G. chiloense* and cultivars including 'FIRE OPAL', 'LADY STRATHEDEN', 'MRS J. BRADSHAW', *G. rivale, G. r.* 'LEONARD'
Helleborus.	*H. niger, H. orientalis*
Heuchera.	*H. sanguinea* (syn. *H.* x *brizoides*), *H.* 'PALACE PURPLE', *H.* 'PEARL DROPS', *H.* 'SCINTILLATION'
Hosta (syn. Funkia).	Small or medium-sized species and hybrids including *H.* 'BLUE MOON' *H. lancifolia, H. undulata, H.* 'WIEHENSTEPHAN'
Incarvillea.	*I. delavayi, I. mairei*
Liatris.	*L. spicata, L. s.* 'ALBA', *L. s.* 'KOBOLD'
Limonium.	*L. latifolium* (syn. *L. platyphyllum*)
Lychnis.	*L. flos-jovis, L. f.* 'HORT'S VARIETY'
Lysimachia.	*L. ephemerum*
Lythrum.	*L. salicaria* 'FIRECANDLE', *L. s.* 'ROBERT', *L. virgatum* 'ROSE QUEEN', *L.v.* 'THE ROCKET'
Morina.	*M. longifolia*
Penstemon.	Hybrids including 'APPLE BLOSSOM', 'GARNET' (syn. 'ANDENKEN AN FRIEDRICH HAHN'), 'KING GEORGE', 'SCHOENHOLZERI' (syn. 'RUBY'), 'SNOW STORM'
Platycodon.	*P. grandiflorus, P. g. albus, P. g. mariesii*
Polemonium.	*P. foliosissimum*
Potentilla.	*P.* 'FLAMENCO', *P.* 'GIBSON'S SCARLET', *P.* 'GLOIRE DE NANCY', *P. nepalensis* 'MISS WILLMOTT', *P. n.* 'ROXANA', *P. rupestris, P.* 'YELLOW QUEEN' and other hybrids

Primula.	*P. auricula* hybrids, *P. denticulata*, *P. vulgaris* and hybrids
Pulsatilla.	*P. alpina* subsp. *apiifolia* (syn. *P. a.* subsp. *sulphurea*), *P. vulgaris* and cultivars
Ranunculus.	*R. aconitifolius* 'FLORE PLENO'
Salvia.	*S. nemorosa* 'LUBECCA', *S. n.* 'EAST FRIESLAND'
Saxifraga.	*S.* x *urbium*
Scabiosa.	*S.* 'BLUE BUTTERFLY', *S. caucasica*, *S. c.* 'CLIVE GREAVES', *S. c.* 'MISS WILLMOTT', *S. c.* 'MOERHEIM BLUE', *S. c.* 'MOONSTONE', *S.* 'PINK MIST', *S. rumelica* (syn. *Knautia macedonica*)
Sedum.	*S.* 'AUTUMN JOY', *S.* 'RUBY GLOW', *S. spectabile* 'BRILLIANT'
Smilacina.	*S. racemosa*
Solidago.	*S. canadensis*, *S.* 'GOLDEN BABY' (syn. 'GOLDKIND'). *S.* 'LENA', *S.* 'QUEENIE' (syn. 'GOLDEN THUMB'), *S.* 'LEMORE' (now classified under x *Solidaster luteus*)
Stachys.	*S. macrantha*, *S. m.* 'ROSEA', *S. m.* 'SUPERBA', *S. m.* 'VIOLACEA'
Trillium.	*T. erectum*, *T. grandiflorum*, *T. sessile*
Trollius.	*R.* x *cultorum* cultivars including 'CANARY BIRD', 'ORANGE PRINCESS', 'SALAMANDER', *T. europaeus*
Veratrum.	*V. album*, *V. nigrum*
Veronica.	*V. gentianoides*, *V. spicata*, *V. s.* 'Alba', *V. s.* 'RED FOX' (syn. 'ROTFUCHS') and other cultivars

❧ PLANTS LISTED IN THE BORDERLINE DIRECTORY ❧

Achillea.	*A.* 'MOONSHINE', *A. taygetea*
Agapanthus.	*A.* Headbourne Hybrids, *A. praecox* subsp. *orientalis* (syn. *A. orientalis*)
Aquilegia.	Hybrids including 'DRAGONFLY', 'MUSIC SERIES HYBRIDS', *A. vulgaris*, *A. v.* 'NORA BARLOW' and other cultivars
Aster.	*A. amellus*, *A. a.* 'KING GEORGE', *A. a.* 'LADY HINDLIP', *A. ericoides*, *A. thompsonii* 'NANUS'
Astilbe.	Species and hybrids
Bergenia.	Hybrids including ABENDGLUT, 'BRESSINGHAM WHITE', 'SILBERLICHT'
Campanula.	*C. lactiflora*, *C. lactiflora* 'LODDON ANNA', *C. latifolia*
Dianthus.	Numerous varieties and hybrids including 'BRYMPTON RED', 'CHARLES MUSGRAVE', 'DAD'S FAVOURITE', 'MRS SINKINS', *D. caryophyllus*
Dicentra.	*D. spectabilis*, *D. s. alba*
Dictamnus.	*D. albus*, *D. a.* var. *purpureus*
Gaillardia.	Hybrids
Gillenia.	*G. trifoliata*
Hosta (syn. Funkia).	Large species and hybrids
Linum.	*L. narbonense*
Lychnis.	*L. chalcedonica*
Monarda.	*M. didyma*
Nepeta.	*N.* x *faassenii*
Paeonia.	*P. lactiflora* and varieties, *P. officinalis*
Phlox.	*P. maculata* and cultivars including 'ALPHA', 'OMEGA'
Sidalcea.	Hybrids including 'CROFTWAY RED', 'LOVELINESS', 'OBERON', 'WILLIAM SMITH'

Sisyrinchium.	*S. striatum*
Tanacetum.	*T. coccineum* and cultivars including 'BRENDA', 'BRESSINGHAM RED'

❧ PLANTS LISTED IN THE SHRUB DIRECTORY ❧

Ballota.	*B. aectabulosa, B. pseudodictamnus*
Caryopteris.	*C.* x *clandonensis, C.* x *c.* 'ARTHUR SIMMONDS', *C.* x *c.* 'KEW BLUE', *C* x *c.* 'HEAVENLY BLUE'
Daphne.	*D. mezereum, D. tangutica* Retusa group
Deutzia.	*D.* x *rosea* 'CAMPANULATA', *D.* x *r.* 'CARMINEA'
Euonymus.	*F. fortunei* and cultivars including 'EMERALD GAIETY', 'EMERALD N' GOLD', 'GOLD TIP', 'SILVER QUEEN', 'SUNSPOT'
Fuchsia.	Hardy species and hybrids including 'ALICE HOFFMAN', 'DISPLAY', 'LADY THUMB', *F. magellanica* var. *gracilis*, 'TOM THUMB'
Gaultheria (syn. Pernettya).	*G. mucronata* and cultivars including 'ALBA', 'BELL'S SEEDLING', 'ROSEA'
Hebe.	*H. albicans, H. armstrongii* 'AUTUMN GLORY', *H. macrantha, H. pinguifolia* 'PAGEI', *H.* 'ROSIE'
Helichrysum.	*H. italicum* (syn. *H. angustifolium*)
Philadelphus.	*P. microphyllus*
Potentilla.	*P. fruticosa* and cultivars including 'ABBOTSWOOD', 'DAYDAWN'. 'ELIZABETH', 'PRINCESS', 'RED ACE', 'ROYAL FLUSH', 'SUNSET', 'TILFORD CREAM'
Ruta.	*R. graveolens, R. g.* 'JACKMAN'S BLUE'
Santolina.	*S. chamaecyparissus* (syn. *S. incana*)
Skimmia.	*S. japonica* and cultivars and subspecies including 'FRAGANS', 'FRUCTUALBO', subsp. *reevsiana*, 'RUBELLA'
Virburnum.	*V. carlesii, V. opulus* 'COMPACTUM'

❧ PLANTS LISTED IN THE BULB DIRECTORY ❧

Allium.	*A. aflatunense, A. giganteum*
Brodiaea (syn. Triteleia).	*B. coronaria, B. laxa* and other species
Camassia.	*C. leichtlinii, C. quamash*
Cyclamen.	*C. coum* (syn. *C. ibericum, C. orbiculatum, C. vernum*), *C. hederifolium* (syn. *C. neapolitanum*), *C. h. album, C. purpurascens*
Erythronium.	*E. californicum* 'WHITE BEAUTY', *E. dens-canis, E.* 'PAGODA', *E. revolutum*
Fritillaria.	*F. meleagris, F. m. alba, F. pallidiflora, F. pontica*
Galtonia.	*G. candicans*
Gladiolus.	*G. byzantinus*
Iris.	Dutch Xiphium hybrids
Leucojum.	*L. aestivum*
Narcissus.	Miniature varieties including 'HAWERA', 'MINNOW', 'TÊTE-À-TÊTE'
Nerine.	*N. bowdenii, N. b.* 'FENWICK'S VARIETY'
Tulipa.	*T. kaufmanniana* and hybrids and other species and hybrids

ᵒ· MAIN DIRECTORY BY HEIGHT ·ᵒ

TALL 75cm (30in) or more	COLOUR	FLOWERING SEASON	HEIGHT
Aconitum 'BRESSINGHAM SPIRE'	violet-blue	midsummer	1-1.2m (3-4ft)
Aconitum x *cammarum* var. *bicolor*	purple-and-white	midsummer	1-1.2m (3-4ft)
Aconitum compactum 'CARNEUM'	salmon-pink	midsummer	1-1.2m (3-4ft)
Aconitum napellus and 'NEWRY BLUE'	indigo-blue/dark blue	midsummer	1-1.2m (3-4ft)
Dierama pendulum and vars	pink	late summer	1-1.5m (3-5ft)
Dierama pulcherrimum and vars	bright pink/white/purple/red	late summer	1-1.5m (3-5ft)
Echinacea purpurea and cvs.	pink shades/white	late summer	60cm-1.2m (2-4ft)
Lysimachia ephemerum	greyish-white	midsummer	1m (3ft)
Lythrum salicaria 'FIRECANDLE'	rose-pink	late summer	60-90cm (24-36in)
Lythrum virgatum cvs.	pink shades	late summer	90cm (36in)
Polemonium foliosissimum	mauve-blue	summer	75cm (30in)
Smilacina racemosa	creamy-white	spring or early summer	60-75cm (24-30in)
Veratrum album and *nigrum*	white/black	mid- to late summer	1-1.2m (3-4ft)

MEDIUM 45-75cm (18-30in)	COLOUR	FLOWERING SEASON	HEIGHT
Armeria pseudoarmeria 'BEES HYBRIDS'	red/pink	early summer	60cm (24in)
Cirsium japonicum	red/pink	mid- to late summer	45-60cm (18-24in)
Coreopsis verticillata	yellow	summer	45-60cm (18-24in)
Diascia rigescens	pink	midsummer	30-50cm (12-20in)
Diascia vigilis	pale pink	midsummer	30-50cm (12-20in)
Doronicum austriacum	bright yellow	spring	45-60cm (18-24in)
Doronicum x *excelsium* cvs.	yellow	spring	60cm (24in)
Erigeron hybrids	lilac/violet/light pink/blue/light mauve-pink	midsummer	45-60cm (18-24in)

Eryngium variifolium	grey, variegated foliage	midsummer	45cm (18in)
Euphorbia polychroma	yellow-green	early spring	45cm (18in)
Filipendula vulgaris and cv.	creamy-white	midsummer	45-60cm (18-24in)
Gentiana asclepiadea	dark blue	mid- to late summer	45-60cm (18-24in)
Hosta medium-sized spp. and hybrids	various colours	midsummer	from 45cm (18in)
Incarvillea delavayi	bright pink	early to midsummer	45-60cm (18-24in)
Liatris spicata and cvs.	pink/red/purple/white	late summer	45-60cm (18-24in)
Lychnis flos-jovis and cv.	purple/pink	early summer	45-60cm (18-24in)
Lythrum salicaria 'ROBERT'	magenta-pink	late summer	75cm (30in)
Morina longifolia	white to pink	midsummer	60-75cm (24-30in)
Penstemon hybrids	red shades/white	midsummer	45-60cm (18-24in)
Platycodon grandiflorus and vars	bluish-purple/white	midsummer	30-60cm (12-24in)
Potentilla spp. and hybrids	red shades/white/yellow	midsummer	45-60cm (18-24in)
Salvia nemorosa 'LUBECCA'	violet-blue	mid- to late summer	45cm (18in)
Ranunculus aconitifolius 'FLORE PLENO'	white	late spring	45-60cm (18-24in)
Scabiosa caucasica cvs.	blue shades/white	mid- to late summer	60cm (24in)
Scabiosa rumelica	dark red	early to late summer	75cm (30in)
Solidago canadensis and hybrids	pale to bright yellow	late summer to autumn	30-60cm (12-24in)
Veronica spicata and cvs.	blue shades/white/pink	early summer	45cm (18in)

SMALL 25-45cm (10-18in)	COLOUR	FLOWERING SEASON	HEIGHT
Aconitum 'IVORINE'	cream	early summer	30-45cm (12-18in)
Anaphalis triplinervis	white	mid- to late summer	30-38cm (12-15in)
Aurinia saxatilis vars. and cvs.	golden/yellow	spring	22-30cm (9-12in)
Brunnera macrophylla	bright blue	spring	30-45cm (12-18in)
Carlina acaulis caulescens	beige	mid- to late summer	20-45cm (8-18ins)
Celmisia coriacea	white	early summer	30-40cm (12-16in)
Doronicum cordatum	yellow	spring	30cm (12in)
Dodecatheon spp.	pink/red	spring to early summer	20-45cm (8-18in)
Geranium renardii	white	early summer	30cm (12in)
Geum borisii	deep orange	spring	22-45cm (9-18in)
Geum chiloense and cvs.	yellow/red shades	early to midsummer	22-45cm (9-18in)
Geum rivale	red, yellow and pink	spring	22-45cm (9-18in)
Geum rivale 'LEONARD'	copper-gold	spring	22-45cm (9-18in)
Helleborus niger	white	winter	30-45cm (12-18in)
Helleborus orientalis forms	many colours	spring	30-45cm (12-18in)
Heuchera sanguinea	coral-red	early summer	30-45cm (12-18in)

Heuchera hybrids	white/pink	early summer	30-45cm (12-18in)
Hosta small spp. and hybrids	various colours	midsummer	from 12-30cm (6-8in)
Incarvillea mairei	pink	early to midsummer	30cm (12in)
Limonium latifolium	lilac	mid- to late summer	30-40cm (12-16in)
Primula auricula hybrids	many colours	spring	15-22cm (6-9in)
Primula denticulata	pink/purple shades/white	spring	15-30cm (6-12in)
Primula vulgaris and hybrids	many colours	spring	15-20cm (6-8in)
Pulsatilla alpina subsp. *apiifolia*	white	spring	15-30cm (6-12in)
Pulsatilla vulgaris and cvs.	pink/red/purple	spring	15-23cm (6-9in)
Salvia nemorosa 'EAST FRIESLAND'	violet-blue	mid- to late summer	75cm (30in)
Saxifraga x *urbium*	pink	early summer	30cm (12in)
Scabiosa 'BLUE BUTTERFLY'	blue	mid- to late summer	20-30cm (8-12in)
Scabiosa 'PINK MIST'	pink	mid- to late summer	20-30cm (8-12in)
Sedum 'AUTUMN JOY'	pink to orange and brown	late summer	45cm (18in)
Sedum 'RUBY GLOW'	maroon	late summer	25cm (10in)
Sedum spectabile 'BRILLIANT'	rose-pink	late summer	45cm (18in)
Stachys macrantha and cvs.	purple and pink shades	midsummer	30-45cm (12-18in)
Trillium erectum	purple-red	spring	30cm (12in)
Trillium grandiflorum	white to pink	spring	30-45cm (12-18in)
Trillium sessile	dark red	spring	15-30cm (6-12in)
Trollius x *cultorum* cvs.	yellow and orange shades	late spring or early summer	30-45cm (12-18in)
Trollius europaeus	yellow	late spring or early summer	30-45cm (12-18in)
Veronica gentianoides	pale blue	spring	20-30cm (8-12in)
Veronica spicata 'RED FOX'	pink-red	early summer	20-25cm (8-10in)

❧ BORDERLINE DIRECTORY BY HEIGHT ☙

TALL 75cm (30in) and above	COLOUR	FLOWERING SEASON	HEIGHT
Agapanthus praecox subsp. *orientalis* and *A.* HEADBOURNE HYBRIDS	blue	midsummer	60-90cm (24-36in)
Aquilegia hybrids and *A. vulgaris* and cvs.	many colours	early to midsummer	15-90cm (12-36in)
Astilbe spp. and hybrids	many colours	summer	30-90cm (12-36in)
Campanula lactiflora and cvs.	lavender-blue/pink	midsummer	1.2-1.5m (4-5ft)

	COLOUR	FLOWERING SEASON	HEIGHT
Campanula latifolia and var.	purple-blue/white	midsummer	1.2m (4ft)
Hosta large spp. and hybrids	various colours	midsummer	90cm (36in) or more
Lychnis chalcedonica	scarlet	early summer	60-90cm (24-36in)
Monarda didyma	red/pink/white	early to late summer	60-90cm (24-36in)
Paeonia spp. and vars.	many colours	early summer	60-90cm (24-36in)
Phlox maculata and cvs.	pink/white	mid- to late summer	60-90cm (24-36in)
Sidalcea hybrids	red/pink shades	mid- to late summer	75-90cm (30-36in)
Tanacetum coccineum and cvs.	red shades	early summer	60-90cm (24-36in)

MEDIUM 45-75cm (18-30in)	COLOUR	FLOWERING SEASON	HEIGHT
Achillea 'MOONSHINE'	bright yellow	midsummer	60cm (24in)
Achillea taygetea	lemon-yellow	midsummer	45cm (18in)
Aquilegia hybrids and *A. vulgaris* and cvs.	many colours	early to midsummer	15-90cm (12-36in)
Aster amellus and cvs.	violet blue/pink	autumn	50cm (20in)
Aster ericoides	white	late autumn	45-60cm (18-24in)
Aster thompsonii 'NANUS'	lavender-blue	autumn	45cm (18in)
Astilbe spp. and hybrids	many colours	summer	30-90cm (12-36in)
Dicentra spectabilis and *alba*	pink-and-white/white	early summer	75cm (30in)
Dictamnus albus and var.	white/pink striped red	midsummer	60cm (24in)
Gaillardia hybrids	many colour combinations	summer	60-75cm (24-30in)
Gillenia trifoliata	white	midsummer	60cm (24in)
Linum narbonense	bright blue	early summer	30-60cm (12-24in)
Sisyrinchium striatum	creamy-white striped purple	early to midsummer	60cm (24in)
Tanacetum coccineum and cvs.	red shades	early summer	60-90cm (24-36in)

SMALL 45cm (18in) and below	COLOUR	FLOWERING SEASON	HEIGHT
Bergenia 'ABENDGLUT'	rosy-red	spring	30-38cm (12-15in)
Bergenia 'BRESSINGHAM WHITE'	white	spring	30cm (12in)
Bergenia 'SILBERLICHT'	white to pink	spring	23cm (9in)
Dianthus old fashioned and modern pinks	many colours	mid- to late summer	25-38cm (10-15in)
Dianthus caryophyllus	dull purple	mid- to late summer	23cm (9in)
Nepeta x *faassenii*	pale lavender-blue	early summer	30-45cm (12-18in)

•• SHRUB DIRECTORY BY HEIGHT ••

d = deciduous   e = evergreen

TALL over 1m (3ft)	COLOUR	FLOWERING SEASON	HEIGHT
Caryopteris x *clandonensis* and cvs. d	grey-green bright blue	late summer	60cm-1.2m (2-4ft)
Daphne mezereum d	grey-green purple/pink	winter	to 1.5m (5ft)
Deutzia x *rosea* cvs. d	dark green rose-pink/white	summer	90cm (3ft)
Euonymus fortunei and cvs. e	various, variegated inconspicuous	summer	to 3m (10ft)
Fuchsia hardy spp. and hybrids d	dark/mid-green various colours	summer to autumn	to 2.2m (7ft) many smaller
Potentilla fruticosa and cvs. d	bright green various colours	summer	60cm-1.2m (2-4ft)
Skimmia japonica and cvs. and subsp. e	dark green white/red spring white/red berries	autumn	1-1.5m (3-5ft)
Viburnum carlesii d	dark green white black fruits autumn	spring	1-1.2m (3-4ft)
Viburnum opulus 'COMPACTUM' d	deep green white berries red autumn	spring	1.5m (5ft)

SMALL below 1m (3ft)	COLOUR	FLOWERING SEASON	HEIGHT
Ballota acetabulosa d	woolly grey-green white	midsummer	60cm (24in)
Ballota pseudodictamnus d	woolly grey-green white	midsummer	60cm (24in)
Daphne tangutica RETUSA GROUP e	glossy purple buds/pinky-white	late spring	60-90cm (24-36in)
Gaultheria mucronata and cvs. e	glossy dark green white prickly spring berries of various colours	autumn	60-90cm (24-36in)
Hebe albicans e	blue-grey white	midsummer	60cm (24in)
Hebe armstrongii 'Autumn Glory' e	deep green violet purple	late summer to autumn	60–90cm (24–36in)
Hebe macrantha e	bright green white	early summer	60cm (24in)
Hebe pinguifolia 'PAGEI' e	grey-green white	early summer	20-24in (8-10in)
Hebe 'ROSIE' e	pink	early to midsummer	30cm (12in)
Helichrysum italicum e	silver-grey mustard-yellow	midsummer	60cm (24in)
Philadelphus microphyllus d	green white	summer	60-90cm (24-36in)

Potentilla fruticosa and cvs. d	bright green various colours	summer	60cm-1.2m (2-4ft)
Ruta graveolens and cv. e	greyish-blue yellow	early to midsummer	30-60cm (12-24in)
Santolina chamaecyparissus e	white-green bright yellow	midsummer	45-60cm (18-24in)

☙ BULB DIRECTORY BY HEIGHT ❧

TALL over 75cm (30in)	COLOUR	FLOWERING SEASON	HEIGHT
Allium aflatunense	purple-red	early summer	75cm (30in)
Allium giganteum	purple-red	early summer	1m (3ft)
Camassia leichtlinii	blue/white/purple	midsummer	1m (3ft)
Camassia quamash	blue/white/purple	midsummer	75cm (30in)
Galtonia candicans	white	mid- to late summer	1-1.2m (3-4ft)

SMALL under 75cm (30in)	COLOUR	FLOWERING SEASON	HEIGHT
Brodiaea coronaria	purple-blue	early summer	30-45cm (12-18in)
Brodiaea laxa	purple-blue	early summer	10-15cm (4-20in)
Cyclamen coum	red/pink/white	midwinter to early spring	7cm (3in)
Cyclamen hederifolium and var.	mauve-pale pink/white	midsummer to mid-autumn	10cm (4in)
Cyclamen purpurascens	red	mid- to late summer	10cm (4in)
Erythronium californicum 'WHITE BEAUTY'	white	spring	15-35cm (6-14in)
Erythronium dens-canis	pinky-purple	spring	10-15cm (4-6in)
Erythronium 'PAGODA'	pale yellow	spring	25-35cm (10-14in)
Erythronium revolutum	white/purple/pink	spring	30-45cm (12-18in)
Fritillaria meleagris and var.	white/purple	spring	30-45cm (12-18in)
Fritillaria pallidiflora	greenish-yellow	spring	30-38cm (12-15in)
Fritillaria pontica	green	spring	45cm (18in)
Gladiolus byzantinus	wine-red	early summer	45cm (18in)
Iris Dutch Xiphium hybrids	white/blue/purple	midsummer	45cm (18in)
Leucojum aestivum	white	late spring	45-60cm (18-24in)
Narcissus miniature vars.	yellow shades	spring	15-25cm (6-10in)
Nerine bowdenii and cv.	pink	autumn	45-60cm (18-24in)
Tulipa species and hybrids	many colours	spring	to 60cm (24in)

◦• MAIN DIRECTORY BY SEASON •◦

+ = continues flowering beyond season

WINTER	COLOUR AND SIZE
Helleborus niger	white + small

EARLY TO MID SPRING	COLOUR AND SIZE
Aurina saxatilis vars. and cvs.	golden/yellow + small
Brunnera macrophylla	bright blue small
Dodecatheon spp.	pink/red small
Doronicum austriacum	bright yellow medium
Doronicum cordatum	yellow small
Doronicum x *excelsum* cvs.	yellow medium
Euphorbia polychroma	yellow-green medium
Helleborus orientalis forms	many colours + small
Primula auricula hybrids	many colours + small
Primula denticulata	pink/purple shades/white small
Primula vulgaris and hybrids	many colours + small
Pulsatilla alpina subsp. *apiifolia*	white small
Pulsatilla vulgaris and cvs.	pink/red/purple small
Trillium erectum	purple-red small
Trillium grandiflorum	white to pink small
Trillium sessile	dark red small

LATE SPRING	COLOUR AND SIZE
Geum borisii	deep orange small
Geum rivale	red, yellow and pink small
Geum rivale 'LEONARD'	copper-gold small
Ranunculus aconitifolius 'FLORE PLENO'	white medium

Smilacina racemosa	creamy-white tall
Trollius europaeus	yellow late spring small
Trollius x *cultorum* cvs.	yellow and orange shades small
Veronica gentianoides	pale blue small

EARLY SUMMER	COLOUR AND SIZE
Aconitum 'IVORINE'	cream small
Armeria pseudoarmeria 'BEES HYBRIDS'	red/pink + medium
Celmisia coriacea	white small
Geranium renardii	white small
Geum chiloense and cvs.	yellow/red shades + small
Heuchera sanguinea	coral-red small
Heuchera hybrids	white/pink small
Incarvillea delavayi	bright pink medium
Incarvillea mairei	pink small
Lychnis flos-jovis and cv.	purple/pink medium
Potentilla spp. and hybrids	red shades/white/yellow medium
Saxifraga x *urbium*	pink small
Scabiosa rumelica	dark red medium
Veronica spicata and cvs.	blue shades/white/pink medium
Veronica spicata 'RED FOX'	pink-red small

MIDSUMMER	COLOUR AND SIZE
Aconitum 'BRESSINGHAM SPIRE'	violet-blue tall
Aconitum x *cammarum* var. *bicolor*	purple-and-white tall
Aconitum compactum 'CARNEUM'	salmon-pink tall
Aconitum napellus	indigo-blue + small
Aconitum 'NEWRY BLUE'	dark blue tall
Anaphalis triplinervis	white + small
Carlina acaulis caulescens	beige + small
Cirsium japonicum	red/pink + medium
Coreopsis verticillata	yellow medium
Diascia rigescens	pink + medium
Diascia vigilis	pale pink + medium
Erigeron hybrids	lilac/violet/light pink/blue/ light mauve-pink + medium
Eryngium variifolium	grey, variegated foliage + medium
Filipendula vulgaris and cv.	creamy-white medium
Gentiana asclepiadea	dark blue medium
Hosta small spp. and hybrids	various colours small
Hosta medium-sized spp. and hybrids	various colours medium
Limonium latifolium	lilac + small
Lysimachia ephemerum	greyish-white tall
Morina longifolia	white to pink medium

	COLOUR AND SIZE
Penstemon hybrids	red shades/white + medium
Platycodon grandiflorus and vars.	bluish-purple/white medium
Polemonium foliosissimum	mauve-blue tall
Salvia nemorosa 'LUBECCA'	violet-blue + medium
Salvia nemorosa 'EAST FRIES-LAND'	violet-blue + small
Scabiosa 'BLUE BUTTERFLY'	blue + small
Scabiosa 'PINK MIST'	pink + small
Scabiosa caucasica cvs.	blue shades/white + medium
Stachys macrantha and cvs.	purple/pink shades small
Veratrum album	white + tall
Veratrum nigrum	black + tall

LATE SUMMER	COLOUR AND SIZE
Dierama pendulum and vars.	pink tall
Dierama pulcherrimum and vars.	bright pink/white/purple/red tall
Echinacea purpurea and cvs.	pink shades/white tall
Lythrum salicaria 'FIRECAN-DLE'	rose-pink tall
Lythrum salicaria 'ROBERT'	magenta-pink tall
Lythrum virgatum cvs.	pink shades tall
Liatris spicata and cvs.	pink/red/purple/white medium
Sedum 'AUTUMN JOY'	pink to orange and brown small
Sedum 'RUBY GLOW'	maroon small
Sedum spectabile 'BRILLIANT'	rose-pink small
Solidago canadensis and hybrids	pale to bright yellow medium

❧ BORDERLINE DIRECTORY ❧ BY SEASON

SPRING	COLOUR AND SIZE
Bergenia 'ABENDGLUT'	rosy-red small
Bergenia 'BRESSINGHAM WHITE'	white small
Bergenia 'SILBERLICHT'	white to pink small

EARLY SUMMER	COLOUR AND SIZE
Aquilegia hybrids and A. vulgaris and cvs.	many colours medium
Dicentra spectabilis	pink-and-white medium
Linum narbonense	bright blue + medium
Lychnis chalcedonica	scarlet tall
Monarda didyma	red/pink/white tall
Nepeta x faassenii	pale lavender-blue + small
Paeonia spp. and vars.	many colours tall
Sisyrinchium striatum	creamy-white, striped purple + medium
Tanacetum coccineum and cvs.	red shades medium

MIDSUMMER	COLOUR AND SIZE
Achillea taygetea	lemon-yellow medium
Achillea 'MOONSHINE'	bright yellow medium
Agapanthus praecox subsp. orientalis and A. HEADBOURNE HYBRIDS	blue tall
Astilbe spp. and hybrids	many colours tall
Campanula lactiflora and cvs.	lavender-blue/pink tall
Campanula latifolia and var.	blue-purple/white tall
Dianthus old fashioned and modern pinks	many colours + small

	COLOUR AND SIZE
Dianthus caryophyllus	dull purple + small
Dictamnus albus and var.	white/pink striped red medium
Gaillardia hybrids	many colour combinations + medium
Gillenia trifoliata	white medium
Hosta large spp. and hybrids	various colours tall
Phlox maculata and cvs.	pink/white tall
Sidalcea hybrids	red/pink shades tall

AUTUMN	COLOUR AND SIZE
Aster amellus and cvs.	violet-blue/pink medium
Aster ericoides	white medium
Aster thompsonii 'NANUS'	lavender-blue medium

◦· SHRUB DIRECTORY BY SEASON ·◦

d = deciduous e = evergreen

WINTER-SPRING/ALL YEAR	COLOUR AND SIZE
Daphne mezereum d	grey-green purple/pink tall
Daphne tangutica RETUSA GROUP e	glossy purple buds/pinky-white small
Euonymus fortunei and cvs. e	various, variegated inconspicuous tall
Gaultheria mucronata and cvs. e	prickly glossy dark green white spring berries of various colours autumn small
Skimmia japonica and cvs. and subsp. e	dark green white/red spring white/red berries autumn tall
Virbunum carlesii d	dark green white spring black fruits autumn tall
Viburnum opulus 'COMPACTUM' d	deep green white spring red berries autumn tall

SUMMER/ALL YEAR	COLOUR AND SIZE
Hebe albicans e	blue-grey white small
Hebe armstrongii 'AUTUMN GLORY' e	deep green violet-purple small
Hebe macrantha e	bright green white small
Hebe pinguifolia 'PAGEI' e	grey-green white small
Hebe 'ROSIE'	grey-green white small
Helichrysum italicum e	silver-grey mustard-yellow small

SUMMER	COLOUR AND SIZE
Ballota acetabulosa d	woolly grey-green white small
Ballota pseudodictamnus d	woolly grey-green white small
Caryopteris x *clandonensis* and cvs. d	grey-green bright blue tall
Deutzia x *rosea* cvs. d	dark green rose-pink/white tall
Fuchsia hardy spp. and hybrids d	dark/mid-green various colours + tall
Philadelphus microphyllus d	green white small
Potentilla fruticosa and cvs. d	bright green various colours + tall
Ruta graveolens and cv. e	greyish-blue yellow small
Santolina chamaecyparissus e	white-green bright yellow small

❦ BULB DIRECTORY BY SEASON ❧

SPRING	COLOUR AND SIZE
Cyclamen coum	red/pink/white midwinter + small
Erythronium californicum	'White Beauty' white small
Erythronium dens-canis	pinky-purple small
Erythronium 'PAGODA'	pale yellow small
Erythronium revolutum	white/purple/pink small
Fritillaria meleagris and var.	white/purple small
Fritillaria pallidiflora	greenish-yellow small
Fritillaria pontica	green small
Leucojum aestivum	white small
Narcissus miniature vars.	yellow shades small
Tulipa species and hybrids	many colours small

SUMMER	COLOUR AND SIZE
Allium aflatunense	purple-red tall
Allium giganteum	purple-red tall
Brodiaea coronaria	purple-blue small
Brodiaea laxa	purple-blue small
Camassia leichtlinii	blue/white/purple tall
Camassia quamash	blue/white/purple tall
Cyclamen hederifolium	and var. mauve-pale pink/ white + small
Cyclamen purpurascens	red small
Galtonia candicans	white tall
Gladiolus byzantinus	wine-red small
Iris Dutch Xiphium hybrids	white/blue/purple small

AUTUMN	COLOUR AND SIZE
Nerine bowdenii and cv.	pink small

USEFUL ADDRESSES AND BOOKS

Royal Horticultural Society, Vincent Square, London SW1P 2PE.

Membership not only brings a monthly magazine, but also entitles you to advice and information from some of Britain's finest horticultural experts. The Royal Horticultural Society also publishes many books, among them **The Plant Finder**, an invaluable annual guide to who is selling what plants, complete with addresses of suppliers, lists of National Collections and up-to-date nomenclature. A booklet entitled **Award of Garden Merit Plants** (1993) lists plants awarded by the RHS for their outstanding excellence for garden decoration or use.

The National Trust Membership Department, P.O. Box 39, Bromley, Kent, BR1 1NH.

The National Trust owns many beautiful gardens, most of which are open to the public several days a week from the beginning of April to the end of October.

Hardy Plant Society, Little Orchard, Great Comberton Pershore, Worcestershire, WR10 3DP.

Very useful for exchange of information and seed, over the last few years the Hardy Plant Society has been responsible for the reintroduction of a number of rare and interesting plants.

National Council for the Conservation of Plants and Gardens (NCCPG), The Pines, RHS Garden, Wisley, Woking, Surrey GU23 6QB.

The NCCPG is responsible, among other things, for the National Collections. these are single genus collections being grown in one place. These collections not only ensure the survival of rare and endangered species, but also provide a perfect chance to observe the often wide variety of species within a genus. From the point of view of the 'Easy Border' gardener it allows you to see which are well behaved and which are more rampant, before buying.

The Cottage Garden Society, Brandon, Ravenshall, Betley, Cheshire CW3 9BH.

Dedicated to preserving the tradition of the cottage garden, this society offers plenty of practical advice on obtaining and growing cottage garden plants.

Reader's Digest Encyclopedia of Garden Plants and Flowers (Reader's Digest 1987, reprinted 1993).

Although it is over twenty years since this book was first printed, new editions have ensured it stays up-to-date and, listing over 3,000 garden plants, it is still one of the 'bibles' for gardeners.

Gardeners' Encyclopedia of Plants and Flowers (Dorling Kindersley, 1989, in association with the RHS).

One of the best features of this book is the photographs, which are helpful for identification as well as inspiration.

Perennials Vols 1 and 2 Roger Phillips and Martyn Rix (Pan 1994).

These contain information on a wide range of plants, all expertly photographed.

Perennial Garden Plants for the modern Florilegium Graham Stuart Thomas (J.M. Dent, revised 1986, in association with the RHS).

An authoritative book, recognised as a standard for all those interested in growing perennials.

Gardener's Latin Bill Neal (Robert Hale).

Useful if you want to understand more about nomenclature and learn why plants have the names they do.

The Month-by-Month Series (David & Charles).

A collection of useful practical books by respected authors on specific gardening subjects including: The Wildlife Garden, The Herb Garden, The Garden in Flower, The Container Garden, and the Easy Garden.

Gardens of England and Wales.

The 'Yellow Book', published annually by the National Gardens Scheme Charitable Trust. This is a guide to open days at over 3000 private gardens, most of which are not normally open to the public. Visiting other gardens is a marvellous way of learning from other people's successes and failures. Most of the gardens also have a selection of plants on sale and you have the benefit of being able to see them growing before making your purchase. Smaller leaflets on individual counties are also available locally.

ACKNOWLEDGEMENTS

I would like to thank all those who have assisted with the creation of this book, including Alasdair Sutherland, the staff of the Royal Botanic Garden, Edinburgh, my husband Roger Ephraums, and Mrs Margaret Ogilvie for permission to photograph House of Pitmuies Garden. My special thanks also to Nora Craig, for her expert advice, and to Jo Weeks, my editor, for her help and hard work.

House of Pitmuies Garden, Angus, Scotland is open daily from 1 April to 31 October, 10am–5pm. Entrance fee.

PHOTOGRAPHS

Jacket: *(front)* The garden at Sticky Wicket, Dorset – Clive Nichols; *(back top)* Justyn Willsmore, *(back middle and bottom)* Garden Picture Library.

Inside pages 6, 17, 30, 36, 39, 64, 67, 68, 70, 74, 75, 77, 84, 85, 89, 90, 91, 101, 104, 114, 115, 118 Garden Picture Library; pages 97, 112 Clive Nichols; all other photographs Justyn Willsmore.

ILLUSTRATIONS
All by Eva Melhuish except pp 60–63 by Avis Murray.

INDEX

Entries in **bold** indicate main entry in the Plant Directories
Entries in *italic* indicate illustrations